The Complete Pool Manual for Homeowners & Professionals

A Step-By-Step Maintenance Guide

By

Dan Hardy

The Complete Pool Manual for Homeowners & Professionals
A Step-By-Step Maintenance Guide

1210 SW 23rd Place • Ocala, Florida 34474 • Phone 800-814-1132 • Fax 352-622-5836
Web site: www.atlantic-pub.com • E-mail: sales@atlantic-pub.com
SAN Number: 268-1250

ISBN-13: 978-1-60138-022-7 ISBN-10: 1-60138-022-4

Library of Congress Cataloging-in-Publication Data

Hardy, Dan J., 1953-
The Complete Pool Manual for Homeowners and Professionals:
a step-by-step maintenance guide / Author: Dan J. Hardy.
p. cm.
Includes bibliographical references and index.
ISBN-13: 978-1-60138-022-7 (alk. paper)
ISBN-10: 1-60138-022-4 (alk. paper)
1. Swimming Pools--Maintenance and repair-- Handbooks, manuals, etc.
United States. I. Title.

TH4763.H37. .2007
643'.5560288--dc22

2007011552

EDITOR: Marie Lujanac • mlujanac817@yahoo.com
PROOFREADER: Angela C. Adams • angela.c.adams@hotmail.com
ART DIRECTION: Meg Buchner • megadesn@mchsi.com
INTERIOR DESIGN: Michelle Bennett • mbennettdesign@yahoo.com

Printed on Recycled Paper

Printed in the United States

We recently lost our beloved pet "Bear," who was not only our best and dearest friend but also the "Vice President of Sunshine" here at Atlantic Publishing. He did not receive a salary but worked tirelessly 24 hours a day to please his parents. Bear was a rescue dog that turned around and showered myself, my wife Sherri, his grandparents Jean, Bob and Nancy and every person and animal he met (maybe not rabbits) with friendship and love. He made a lot of people smile every day.

We wanted you to know that a portion of the profits of this book will be donated to The Humane Society of the United States.

–Douglas & Sherri Brown

TABLE OF

Contents

Chapter 3: Water Chemistry 73

Chapter 4: Cleaning The Pool 87

Chapter 5: Chemicals and Cures 107

Chapter 6: Pool Problems 133

Acknowledgements

Thanks to my wife, Carol, my daughter, Marci, and my sons, Matthew and Michael, for putting up with me and helping me improve my business by sacrificing their time and fun for my "Beating-Mother-Nature" obsession.

I would like to thank Brett Heffelfinger for helping me for years with the technical data and assistance with new products that came on the market. His advice and knowledge I still use on a daily basis.

I want to thank Rick Lorick for letting an old, fat man get back into the business and not only learn and have hands-on experience with the newest equipment and the most elite pools in the area, but also letting me have fun in an industry doing what I love. His pools are a delight to work on and they are some of the most sophisticated systems in Florida.

Thanks to John Bromley who inspired me to restart this book again after I gave up a few years ago. He is the most technically knowledgeable man I have ever met. His knowledge is endless. He also falls into pools as gracefully as I do.

Finally, thanks to my present and past pool customers wherever you are. I appreciate the chance to make your pools enjoyable. The smiles on your faces far surpass any monetary rewards I have received.

Dan Hardy
Ocala, Florida
March 2007

Foreword

I have known Dan Hardy for more than 10 years. In my capacity as President of the North Central Florida Chapter of the Florida Swimming Pool Association, Inc., (FSPA). I teach pool professionals and private pool owners how to design and maintain pools. As such, I have the deepest respect for Dan's professionalism, hard work, thirst for knowledge, and now, in this book, his ability to make a complicated subject easily understandable.

Dan and I work in a state that has the most year-round swimming pools and which suffers, along with the rest of the country, from a lack of skilled, licensed pool technicians. Only one college in Florida offers training in aquatics technology, and there are no vocational-technical programs, no apprenticeship programs, and few associations to contact for information. As a result, a nationwide network of professionals has developed who are well-known for their expertise, the FSPA and the Association of Pool and Spa Professionals (APSP). Dan Hardy stands with the best of them.

He literally started his career as a child, helping his dad take care of pools, and his work is top-notch. He is the "go to" pool doctor for both owners of small above-ground pools and owners of huge "party pools" in North Central Florida. His customers include our friend, John Travolta, and well-known retired sports figures. They know they can rely on Dan because of his intense desire for perfection, chemical and electrical safety, and beauty of operation in an ever-changing industry.

New products, new designs, new building materials, and new computerized technologies enter the pool field every year, creating a vacuum of information for both the everyday pool owner and the professional.

That is why Dan has compiled this book, which I find superior to any on the market, not just because it was written by an extremely wise, good friend but because its language is everyday English. Even with no knowledge of the intricacies of pools, anyone can follow his safety precautions concerning electricity and hazardous chemicals, which I consider the most valuable part of this book. The reader is caught up in his enthusiasm for his work and his joy in turning a "bad" pool into a happy center of family fun.

Whether you are contemplating having a pool of your own, having a pool business of your own, or you are already in the pool industry in any capacity, this book should be your chosen guide and reference. Dan's excellent ability to grasp new technology quickly and translate it into a step-by-step, logical, workable, safe procedure is an enviable trait in a writer. He is a natural teacher and a true professional, and his book not only fills a void but, I believe, sets a new standard for the presentation of vocational information.

Randolph W. Taylor, Jr., CPO
R.W. Taylor Design and Consulting, Inc.
Cells: 352-427-9928 and 352-583-5243
E-mail: *rt4pools1@Earthlink.net*

Introduction

This book was written for every pool owner to understand the basics of pools and spas, and how to maintain and repair them, and it is intended as well for all pool service and maintenance people who need to perform their jobs in a safe and professional manner. It is not intended for pool builders although they should have a copy to consult when treating pool water.

For the pool owner, it is fairly easy to maintain a single pool. Once the curing process is over, which can take from 12 to 18 months (yes, pool finishes still cure for that long), you just have to learn what your water likes and how it reacts. I have always said that having a pool is like having a child: you have to pay it some attention every day if only for a few minutes, depending on a number of items, which we will get into later. You do have to learn what Mother Nature will do to your pool or spa, and you must find a prevention and a cure. You may have observed that different pool professionals have different opinions, use different products, and all have their own way of doing things to achieve the goal of good, clean, safe water.

For the pool professional, I will help guide you so that you can do your job more efficiently and provide you with that good feeling of taking something that can be harmful and making it nice. It always helps to get a second opinion and hear how to deal with certain problems that can come up. For the aspiring or new pool professional, this book is a great place to start for a successful career and a good living.

Almost every product made for your pool's water is poison.

Because of that, be sure that you add only what you need and remember that one product most likely will throw something else off kilter in your pool. Knowing this will separate you from the people who think they know and the ones that do know. I do honestly believe it is an art and a science.

My belief is that most water problems can be prevented and that the water in your pool can be maintained safely. If you do your best to prevent problems with your water, the fewer chemicals need to be added, depending on your water source.

It starts deceptively simply with basic testing and attempts to balance water. That is the start. There is nothing that you cannot correct in water, although sometimes draining and replacement may be more cost efficient than treatment, and it may be required for certain problems, especially in spas, where the water volume is low.

Every pool is different. Each has its own characteristics due to source water, materials used to construct the pool, and the equipment, which in my opinion is the most important part of a pool.

This book discusses filtration in detail because of its importance. Part of filtration is flow. The pool must have good flow and must be able to circulate properly and efficiently. That is where the pool builder must know a little more than just basic concrete work.

I will attempt to inform you of some of the most advanced systems and equipment that are available in the industry today. I will also warn you of products that are just designed for the purpose of selling you something that performs poorly. There are many such products out there.

For the pool owner, remember that pool supply stores have one thing on their mind: making money. Their margin for error is usually smaller and it is typical that people who take a water sample a couple of times a week wind up buying something after each test. I will guide you through the process of taking care of your own pool and help you ultimately save money. I have a very simple philosophy. It is better to be in your pool than it is to be working on your pool.

ABOUT ME

For more than 20 years, I have proven that you can control Mother Nature's water that you play in.

In a small town in New Mexico, my father owned a country club that had a commercial pool. It was my job at a fairly early age to keep this pool at certain levels. My father was a frugal man, and to save a dollar we did not always do everything right. Since inspections of pools were limited, no one from the county was going to pop in and test our pool water as long as swimmers were not harmed.

To learn more, I did go to the local library, but books and information were limited and very basic. I thought TDS, which will be covered later in the book, was some new drug older kids used.

Now after many years of trial and error and a lot of research and reading, I have perfected water management. I have some high-end pools, including John Travolta's pool in Florida. It does not matter who owns them just who takes care of them.

THE POOL PROFESSIONAL

I refer in this book to a pool professional. A person who can maintain multiple pools in a safe, controlled, and efficient manner is definitely a professional. It is a job that no one is going to tell you how to do. We can guide you to the basics, but the individual will have to adapt what he or she learns and apply it to the craft. Most courses will give you basic guidelines and nothing more. It is up to the pool owner and the professional to learn how to maintain a certain pool, and the most important thing is to learn everything you can about the products you put into the pool.

Read the instructions. They are put on the containers for a reason, and some will not work unless certain things are done prior to use, such as attaining certain chemical levels. If instructions are not clear to you, call the company that makes the product and ask questions so that you understand. You only learn by asking questions. Also for the professional, if any company offers free classes about their products, go to them. It may not be a product that you use, but you will always learn something about water management that you will eventually apply to some pool. Picking the brains of people in your own business is your best method for learning. You will spot the ones who are bogus and the ones who are honest about what they do and how they do it. Remember, everyone has their own way of doing things, and their way just may help you with a problem. Nowadays with the Internet, it is easier to find good information on maintaining water that is non-corrosive and non-irritating in your pool and spa. Of course, you still have to use your head and experience, but it can be done.

For the professional, be proud of what you do. Most pool owners think that they could maintain pools for a living, but if they were so good, you would not be there taking care of their pools.

POOL HISTORY

Swimming pools date back to 2500 B.C. when swimming became part of the elementary curriculum for Greek and Roman boys. Care of the water consisted of draining and replacing with fresh water. Filtration was not an option.

During the third millennium B.C. in ancient Indus an elaborate ceremonial pool was built called the "Great Bath." It was 7 meters wide and 12 meters long. Its maximum depth was 2.4 meters. It was made of brick and gypsum plaster and was covered with a natural tar called bitumen. The builders must have been the first ones to know about pool surfaces and sealers.

The next large pool was founded by King Pandudhabaya in 437 B.C. in Sri Lanka. It was called the Kuttampokuna. It was a set of elaborately decorated pools that are 51′ wide, and the small pool is 91′ long and the larger pool is 132′ long. Their intended use was to purify the kings. The pool was fed by water that actually went through a rock filtration system. It was the best demonstration of hydrological engineering until that time. The pools were built as bathing pools for the monks of the Abhayagiri Monastery of Anuradhapura also in Sri Lanka. Water actually came out of a lion's head. That was the first "spitter." The water flowed into a pit, where the mud and dirt sank to the bottom guaranteeing a clean water flow to the pools. And we call these people primitive.

If you are truly interested in the history of pools, you can research for days and find many different races and countries that built and used pools. Some were used as public bathing pools and some were intended only for the elite.

It was in the early 1900s when swimming pools started popping up all over the world. Only the rich could afford them, but as time went on and construction practices improved, the backyard pool became commonplace. In colder climates, hot tubs became popular using basic wooden boat construction methods. Since early boats had to be handcrafted to be watertight, adapting the process to a hot tub came naturally. These types of spas were found mostly in the northern United States.

These innovators who built pools or hot tubs in the early 1900s set the stage for what is going on now. Pools have advanced so much in the past few years that the rectangular shape has been supplanted by any shape that any pool designer can imagine. Different types and shapes of pools are included in this book so you can see what I mean. It's time to jump in.

See center insert, photo one – large, modern pool

CHAPTER 1

The Pool

OVERVIEW

A pool is a shell of different kinds of material. Inground pools are mainly constructed with a concrete type product. They are made of gunite, shotcrete, block, or poured cement, all of which are porous so that water can actually seep through these products unless an overcoat of plaster, tile, or other coating is applied. In my opinion, if you are going to paint a pool, you might as well just fill it in and use it as a flower garden. Paint does not last and you need to sandblast it off to remove it. Paint may be used only as a last resort for those who cannot afford to resurface their pool. There are also some products of fiberglass that can be installed over the shell and some are not bad, but the problem with them is usually the installation is poor and they fail. Stick with the proper surface to avoid unhappy swimmers and expensive problems.

CONCRETE POOLS

A concrete pool may be called by other technical terms, but I will refer to it as a concrete pool from here on. Concrete pools start as an idea that goes into a design. They can be made in various shapes and sizes. When designing a concrete pool the owners can actually add their ideas to the shape of the pool. Once the new owner approves the design and colors, it goes to the permit department of your local city or county. Each municipality has certain codes that must be maintained for safety and general requirements to ensure that the pool owner gets a quality product. After the approval from the building department and maybe engineering, it is time to start the pool.

INGROUND LINER POOLS

Liner pools have gone from wood to inground liners that come in different thicknesses, measured in mils. For the small price difference, always choose the thickest liner. Inground liner pools are constructed of many things, but the most common materials are block, steel structures, and pre-made composite panels. Vinyl liners have their advantages and disadvantages.

I have built a couple of inground liner pools from scratch. We used block. Both pools were three feet deep at the shallow end and four and a half feet on the deep end. They had a main drain, seven returns, two skimmers, and a cleaner port. One was a 12′ by 24′ pool and the other was a 16′ by 32′ pool. I tell you this to let you know how simple it was.

We poured a 24″ by 24″ footer around the pool. It was reinforced with four one-half inch rebar around the whole footing. The first layer of block was laid on the inside edge of the footer, and the second layer was laid over the first layer. Rebar was placed every three feet from the footer to the top of the block.

Not only was it cheaper to use the block than to pour a 24″ solid wall, but the process did not require expensive forms.

The inlet pipes and the cleaner port were put through the block before pouring. The skimmers were vinyl liner. The main drain was plumbed through the footer using a larger piece of pipe. We used one and a half inch piping on the pool. That way we could simply slide the main drain line through the pipe in the footer. It was not intended to be permanent in case I ever had to replace it. Vinyl liner return fittings were used and were permanently installed in concrete. That was the hard part. Once all that was done and all the plumbing was complete, we vacuum-tested all lines and backfilled and compacted the soil around the structure. The skimmer was concreted into place so that it would not move. On a liner pool, a plate fits over the liner and is screwed into the skimmer mouth for a seal, and then the liner is cut to let water into the skimmer.

After the walls were up, we had mason sand brought in for the floor at a depth of six inches. This was raked, troweled, compacted, and soaked with water for a few days. Once we had a good bottom we measured it for the liner and ordered it custom made as we do for each pool. The liner had a bead on it that fit into a track that was mounted at the top of the block. So that the rough block would not damage the liner, we glued carpet padding onto the block all around the pool wherever the block was exposed to the liner. Footers were used around the pool as coping and then a deck was poured. This book is not for the builder but shows you how easy it can be to build a basic pool.

FIBERGLASS POOLS

Fiberglass pools are a preformed shell that is delivered on a flatbed truck and lowered in a hole that has been dug, plumbed, leveled, and backfilled in. Some actually can come in pieces to be assembled. Getting them level and stable so they will not shift can be a problem, and I have seen some pools that have moved after the filling process has begun. They also have their advantages and disadvantages.

Fiberglass pools have been around since the 1950s, and the only comparison to structural strength was a personal boat made of fiberglass. With the increasing cost of materials, fiberglass pools are getting more expensive. Their claim is that they do not alter the pH because of the surface of the pool. Calcium levels can be reduced, even though a 200 ppm level of calcium hardness is usually recommended. It is a slicker surface making it harder for algae to take hold. Algae still try to form but will not stick to fiberglass, and an easy brushing does knock it right off. It can be easily repaired and cleaning is easier, too. Fiberglass is a combination of fiber reinforcement and resin. It is stronger than other materials similar in weight and size. Compared to wood, metals, or concrete, it is more durable when exposed to water.

ON-THE-GROUND POOLS (ABOVE GROUND)

The installation of a true on-the-ground pool is a process that requires almost perfect leveling to keep the pool from coming apart and exploding, which can cause serious property damage, injury, and even death. If you choose an on-the-ground pool, please have a professional with a good reputation install it for safety's sake. An on-the-ground pool has the same advantages as a fiberglass pool as far as basic maintenance. However, both are dangerous when algae form because they become very slippery and dangerous.

There is a pool on the market that actually uses air as the wall supports. You inflate it using a blower to fill the pool walls with air and it does support water. It has a better circulation system than most but still is prone to problems if maintenance is not done on a regular schedule. It is more portable since the level of the pool is not as critical as in the on-the-ground pool. Once the grandchildren have left you can actually drain the pool, deflate it, and store it away for the next time—not a bad temporary pool for limited use.

A liner pool is not a lifetime pool since you will have to change the liner after a few years or the first time you stick a pool pole through the liner. Leaks can happen, and the patches are easy to install but they are only a temporarily repair. Basic cleaning can remove a patch on vinyl.

Now we have this shell filled with water. To treat the water in the pool, you have to know how much water is in the pool.

CALCULATING POOL VOLUME

It is hard to believe, but one of the biggest problems with inexperienced pool technicians today is that they cannot do math. There is no gentle way to put it. There are companies that make pool tech math books for teaching pool technicians the necessary math skills needed to measure, calculate volumes, and most important, calculate chemical dosages.

Another problem is that if you go to the Internet and enter pool water calculations, you will get many different mathematical formulas that are confusing. The ones I use here are those I feel are the most accurate since I have compared them to metering water or compared them to the calculations of pool builders who have a program for designing a pool.

The best time to measure volume is while the pool is being filled by using portable meters that can be connected to your water source to measure the amount of water added to the pool. You can also use the meter supplied by the city or water company that will tell you how much water is used. Otherwise figuring the volume will give you the best estimate. You notice the word "estimate." When you figure pool volume, one of the dimensions is the average depth. Since a pool going from the shallow end to the deep end is not a perfect decline, you are estimating water volume.

This is fairly easy:
Length X Width X
the Average Depth X 7.5
= volume in gallons

RECTANGULAR AND SQUARE POOLS

Now you can calculate the same volume using metric measurements and the result will be cubic meters of volume. Some chemicals may give you the dosages in liters instead of gallons, but I have seen it on the container of both gallons and liters, so the metric conversion probably will not be a problem.

The math is fairly simple: the length of the pool X the width of the pool, X the average depth. That is an estimation. Most pools are not of an equal slope from the shallow end to the deep end, so that your calculation is only your best estimate. Then you multiply that number by 7.5 which gives you your total volume of water.

Example: you have a 32′ long pool, that is 16′ wide. The

shallow end is 3 feet deep. The deep end of the pool at the deepest part which usually is close to the main drain is 8 feet. You simply add the three foot and the eight foot which is 11, and then divide it by two. That comes out to be 5.5 feet: your average depth. Now, 32 X 16 equals is 512 which is your square footage of the surface of the pool. You take the 512 square feet and multiply it by the 5.5 average depth, which is 2,816. That number is then multiply by 7.5, and your total volume is 21,120 gallons of water.

FREEFORM, KIDNEY, OR IRREGULAR SHAPED POOLS

Now some people will break up the different shapes of a pool into smaller sections to make it easy for calculation. I have found that unless the pool is a certain depth all over, your estimation gets more risky. An oval pool will be the easiest to calculate with the formula and will be more accurate. When you get into different shapes and kidney pools, your estimate will be off the actual volume because of the shape. The formula that I use for these types of pools is:

Length X Width X
Average Depth X 6.7 = gallons of water

The best way to find out the volume of a kidney or freeform or irregular-shaped pool is to contact the builder. If you cannot, try this formula. 0.45 X (a + b) X length X average depth X 5.9 = gallons of water. A + B is the short width plus the longest widths divided by two to get an average width.

See center insert, photo two – freeform pool

OVAL POOLS

An oval pool that has straight walls with a semicircular end can be calculated as:

Length X Width X Average Depth X 5.9.

ROUND POOLS

I compare this to manufacturers' data and it comes out right. If it is an on-the-ground pool, remember you are measuring the depth of water and not the size of the pool. A 52″ pool, usually only has 48″ of water in it.

Diameter X Diameter X Average Depth X 5.9 = gallons of water.

Let's take a 24′ diameter round on-the-ground pool. It has walls that measure 52″ but only holds 48″ or four feet of water. It has a flat bottom with a slight angle toward the drain but not much.

Okay, 24′ x 24′ = 576 square feet of water. You then multiply the depth of 4′, which equals 2,304. The 2,304 figure is multiplied by 5.9 and you come up with 13,593 gallons of water.

BASIC POOL CONSTRUCTION

This book is designed for maintenance of the pool, and not for building a pool, but I feel that you need some understanding of how it is made to be able to work on it.

The concrete pool is a combination of a concrete product, whether it is gunite, shotcrete, block, or poured concrete walls and floors. In the United States, most pools are made of either gunite or shotcrete. The use of block and poured concrete was in earlier designs, although some builders do use some of these products in specialty pools where it is easier or stronger to use a block or poured concrete on a section of a pool. Since concrete basically has no strength by itself, metal reinforcing rods (rebar) or wire is used to add strength to the concrete. In low temperatures, calcium was used in concrete mixtures to decrease the working and curing time of concrete. It has been determined that calcium, basically salt, eats up metal over time, so most places do not allow you to use calcium in concrete products except where the concrete needs to set up quickly.

After the basic design, the types of equipment, and any special features have been decided on, plans must be submitted to the local planning office for approval. When the plans are approved, a permit for building is issued—for a fee.

Now to put a pool in the ground you have to have a hole shaped precisely to the shape of the pool. After the hole is dug it must be determined that the ground can support the pool. Not only is the shell heavy, but water weighs more than 8.3 pounds per gallon, 62.4 pounds per cubic foot, and 2.2 pounds per liter. A typical 15″ x 30″ concrete pool that has an average depth of 5.5′ holds 18,562 gallons of water that weighs 154,811 pounds. That's a lot of weight. Different procedures are used for different types of soil. Local engineering can establish what procedures need to be followed, and established codes must be met for each pool.

See center insert, photo three - basic rectangular pool

After the hole has been excavated to the shape of the pool, forms are put up to hold the rebar in place along with a wire mesh that has a felt type backing to hold the concrete in place when it is shot. The term shot means using a concrete type pump that sprays the concrete product on the pool. A rectangular pool is easy to get square and straight but the freeform or kidney pools can be a challenge. Workers have to form the concrete to the desired thickness and the correct shape.

Before the concrete is shot, the skimmer(s) must be fitted into the pool, the main drain(s) must be placed and plumbed, all the return lines must be placed in the wall section, and any other equipment or features must be installed or plumbed. Normally before shooting the concrete all piping will be pressure checked to ensure that they do not leak and that all fittings have been properly glued.

After the basic shell is formed, the curing takes place. Different builders prefer letting a shell cure for different lengths of time. Once the proper curing time has taken place, usually the tile is installed on the pool. The tile is not just for looks. If the level of water were to be on just the plaster, you would get a line at the water level all around the pool that is caused by what I am told is hydration of the concrete and plaster. The stains left on the sides without tile would be impossible to clean.

See center insert, photo four – pool under construction

See center insert, photo five – pool under construction

See center insert, photo six – pool under construction

That brings up a very important point. While a pool is filling after construction, it must not have the water stopped for any length of time. The flow must continue until the fill is complete. The customer or owner can turn the water off for showers and doing dishes, but it must be turned back on. A constant rise in the water level until it reaches its proper level is very important to prevent ring. Once you get one, it will be there for the life of the plaster, and even acid washing a pool will not remove it.

Let's back up to the point where the tile set has cured and the plumbing and equipment set have been completed so that the plaster can be applied if the water and power are available at the pool. As soon as the hose goes in, a pool is born. Some plaster installers actually let the pool set overnight, acid wash it with a mild solution to expose the aggregate, and then fill the pool.

This is a new pool being constructed that has had the shell or shotcrete finished and the tiles have been installed. This pool is being cured before the surface is put on and the deck is installed. This is considered to be a free form pool. It is best to try to get the volume for this pool from the builder.

See center insert, photo seven –finished and filled pool

THE FIBERGLASS POOL

Fiberglass pools for the most part are preformed and shipped by truck to the job site. A hole is dug for the shell and the pool is usually lowered into the hole by a crane. When it is in the hole, the plumbing is done and the pool is set and backfilled. I have seen these pools move because of poor soil or pool installation and be unleveled after filling. The only thing good I can say about a fiberglass pool is it is a little cheaper. Due to its slick surface, it resists algae, but on the other hand if algae start to form it can be slick in its early stages and dangerous for those who cannot swim. If the shell is not set properly, it can flex and crack. It can be repaired but will never be the same. I am not a big fan of these pools for many reasons, but many of them do work well. If you live in an area of high water tables, draining a fiberglass pool can be disastrous. It can literally pop out of the ground (and so can concrete pools). It's not a pretty sight. If you are going to drain a pool, you must be informed if you are in an area where this might happen. Call local builders before draining and ask their advice.

ON-THE-GROUND POOLS

Now I do no more work on the on-ground pools or in-ground liner pools, but thousands are sold around the country. The first problem with an above ground pool is the circulation usually is very poor. Remember filtration is the key to a clean and manageable pool. Most above ground pools come with cheap, inefficient pumps and filters. Most are undersized for the pool. If you consider buying an on-the-ground pool, follow these easy procedures. Have your installer put in a main drain. They make drains for liner pools. Also have your installer add an additional pressure return to the opposite side of the pool across from the skimmer so you have good circulation. The addition of an extra suction line for a pool cleaner can also be put in. The standard pool pump that comes with a kit will not do the job.

I used to provide with all my on-the-ground pools (up to a 24′ round pool) a Hayward Max Flo pump with a 900-square-foot cartridge filter or preferably a DE filter, which I will get into later. The purpose of this choice was that it is my professional opinion that you should be in the pool, not working on it. The proper equipment will cost you less in chemicals and save you time. I have seen too many on-the-ground pool owners get disgusted and shut the pool down because they could not maintain it due to poor equipment. The level of an on-the-ground pool is critical. I have seen pools pop out of the lower track and just explode. People have died because of this, and it is extremely important to have the installation done right. Think of this. A 24′ by 48″ round pool holds around 12,600 gallons, which weighs 126,000 pounds. When this water comes out of the side of the pool, whatever is in the pool is going out that hole with that water. Again, not a pretty sight.

One of the major problems with liner pools, whether they are in the ground or on the ground, is the lack of common sense during installation. You cannot put sharp toys or other sharp or pointed things in a liner pool. Sure, they can be patched, but a patch is only a temporary fix.

During installation of one of my last inground liner pools—which, by the way, is good money—the customer called me a couple of weeks after the installation and said her pool was leaking. I went to her home and noticed what looked like small, perfect circles on the bottom of the liner. As the mother went into the house, I asked the children what caused those rings. They told me they were pole-vaulting in the pool with the pool pole. When the mother came back outside, she asked me what it would take to fix it. I told her another $2,500 would take care of it. It was the last time I heard from her. Even cleaning can ruin a liner pool. The professional should never use a hammerhead to clean a liner pool. I learned the hard way. Luckily for me it was only an 18′ diameter on-the-ground pool.

If you bought a pool at your local hardware, Target, or Wal*Mart stores, I feel your pain. Your pool may hold water, but it did not come with anything that I would call a circulation pump and filter, and you will not have it long.

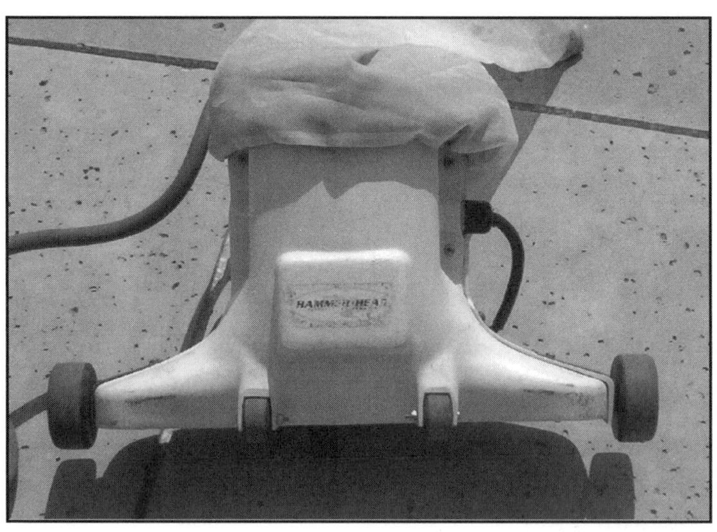

See center insert, photo eight - hammerhead cleaner

BASIC PLUMBING OF POOLS

The average pool consists of a skimmer, a main drain or two, returns, and possibly a cleaner port. It may also have a system that has return heads that actually lift up under pressure of the water and rotate to push the debris on the bottom of the pool so that the main drain can suck these particles out of the pool and send them to the filter. These heads (I call them pop-ups) are installed in the floor and steps of the pool. Good builders add many other items for the newer pools that work more efficiently for proper flow and filtering.

Before the plumbing is done, the volume of water that needs to flow has to be calculated to make sure you size the pipe and equipment properly. When water flows through a pipe, it creates friction. This friction is measured as friction loss or is called resistance. When a fitting, coupling, or anything changes the direct flow of the water, it creates friction or resistance. Friction loss is usually figured in 100 foot of flow.

Let me give you an example. We have a 2-inch line that is 100′ long. We will use only the basic factors to avoid confusion. This 100′ line has a certain amount of resistance. This length of pipe has a certain reduction of flow compared to a 10′ pipe. Whenever the water changes direction, it creates more friction. If in this 100′ pipe you have a 90-degree elbow fitting, it adds 8.6 feet to the length of the pipe as far as measuring the resistance. A tee fitting instead of the elbow would add 12.1 feet to the length of the pipe. When plumbing, it is important to go the straight route. The less you change direction, the better off you will be, and the better flow you will have. These calculations have to be figured when you choose a pump to provide the proper flow measured in gallons per minute. Either too large or too small a pump could result in improper flow.

SKIMMERS

See center insert, photo nine – phantom cleaner

A skimmer is a simple piece of equipment. Its primary job is to clean the surface of the water by creating a sucking action that pulls debris into the skimmer basket and holds it until the basket is empty. The returns can be adjusted to force water toward the skimmer to help with this process. Most new pools generally have two skimmers for cleaning the surface better and for other safety factors. Some skimmers have a door that helps control the flow of water called a "weir." Some skimmers come with a section that fits inside the skimmer basket that floats and it does the same job. That device is called a "floating weir." Depending on the builder, the skimmers, which usually have two threaded holes in the bottom, can be plumbed many ways. Some skimmer lines are "shared" which means that they also feed some other feature through another pump, like a fountain, and overflow for a spa, or some other water feature. Care needs to be taken when adjusting some of these shared lines not to starve a second pump. I do not like shared lines unless a separate function, such as a spa overflow, or some water feature has set limits not to starve another system. Check valves are critical.

Now some pools have no skimmers but have what is called a negative or vanishing edge. It typically makes it look like the water extends to the horizon. As the water level rises, it flows over the edge of the pool and falls into what we refer as the pit, or in some elite pools it can actually flow into another pool where it is picked back up by a pump or two and put back into the pool, and the process continues. The real advantage for the professional is that the pool will almost clean itself.

See center insert, photo ten – vanishing edge

See center insert, photo eleven – vanishing edge (2)

The edge on this pool is actually reversed so that a track for the safety cover can be mounted. As the overflow on the spa spills onto the pool, it takes all the debris that is floating on the surface and dumps it into the pool. Then the pool does the same and dumps it into the pit. With constant flow on both, most debris does not have time to sink. This pool, which is hardly used, is covered most of the time and only a circulation pump is used with the Caretaker system or when pop-ups and the drains on the pit are turned off. When I arrive for my weekly cleaning, I start it up and let it do its thing. While I am taking care of a very nice fountain in the front, two four-horsepower pumps fed by four-inch lines circulate the water from the pit to the pool by four separate lines, two inches in diameter. If you want to see some water movement, this is it. It moves the water so well that it will actually stir up a lot of the debris on the bottom of the pool and shoot it over the side to the pit.

Before I get into the individual parts, I will say that when pools were first being built, some things were plumbed together that we wish were not. Older pools often have one line coming up to the suction side of the pump. What that means is that the skimmer and main drain are plumbed together. With only one valve, it is almost impossible to adjust.

Some of the older pools used a skimmer that had a basket specially designed so that you could turn it to adjust the flow of water. It could shut off the main drain to a certain extent or let both the drain and the skimmer pull water equally. This really was very different from a valve, but it was the best that we got sometimes. A system that had the skimmer and drain plumbed together created problems vacuuming the pool. To increase suction, you had to put something over the drain to stop the flow of water. If all the leaves and debris were on top of the drain cover, you had to turn the pump off, take a brush and remove the debris, start the pump up, and install the cover over the drain. There is a cover designed for this purpose that can be installed and removed by a pool-pole. If you have multiple skimmers that are plumbed together and you need to plug one or both up temporarily, you can use plugs or a tennis ball.

The plumbing of pools has expanded in design and application to be quite sophisticated. With the calculations of various designs and features of a system, plumbing could become an art.

MAIN DRAINS

Main drain refers to the drain or drains that are located in the deep end of the pool. Newer pools for safety reasons will have multiple drains and some will have none. It depends on local regulations and design requirements. Since the residential diving pool of 8′ to 10′ deep is slowly leaving the scene because of insurance reasons, shallow pools are being built at five or six feet deep at the deepest end, allowing for better water circulation and fewer problems.

RETURN LINES

Return lines are simple. Just as they are named, they return the water after it has gone from the pump, through the filter, and through other equipment if installed and then returned to the pool. Usually the returns have adjustable nozzles that let you direct how the water flows.

If proper designs and plumbing are followed, you have no dead spots in the pool. A dead spot is a place where very little or no circulation takes place. These areas are great places for debris to accumulate and algae to form. It is very important in a dead spot that during your cleaning, you brush this section to remove any particles that have attached themselves to the wall of the pool. It will pay off in the end.

CLEANER PORTS

A cleaner port is a separate PVC line that is a designated cleaner line whether it is for suction cleaners or pressure-fed ones using a booster pump. It is very simple.

The following photo is a typical pad for equipment. This pool was remodeled and the original plumbing was used to make an older pool perform better and be operator-friendly. It shows the use of valves and check valves on all lines for the various functions that can be achieved for the effect that one wants. On the left side of the photo there is an electric actuator that, when demanded, changes the water from overflowing from the spa to the pool and makes the spa a self-contained and functioning unit.

This is a typical pad for equipment. This pool was remodeled and the original plumbing was used to make an older pool perform better and be operator-friendly. It shows the use of valves and check valves on all lines for the various functions that can be achieved for the effect that one wants. On the left side of the photo there is an electric actuator that, when demanded, changes the water from overflowing from the spa to the pool and makes the spa a self-contained and functioning unit. The spa was added during the remodeling phase.

The picture above shows a lack of space for any equipment. I call this photo "Not enough space." Inside that small area are three pumps, a cartridge filter, a gas spa heater, a blower for the spa, an off-line tablet chlorinator, and numerous valves that control many functions including water features. This is an example of poor planning in design.

BASIC PIPING

As you notice in the photos white piping is used. That is PVC or polyvinyl chloride pipe. It is chemical and sunlight resistant, easy to use, inexpensive, and was designed to carry unheated water. You will notice that the same pipe is used with the heater. The plumbing that comes out of the heater is a special pipe that is called a heat sink. It simply means that this will absorb the hottest water from the connection before it runs into the PVC pipe. If they are working properly, PVC pipes can endure temperatures of a heated spa.

PVC pipes also come in a flexible form that you will see in portable spas and sometimes used in building pools. Normally it does have the strength and durability as the hard pipe and is usually not used in areas where if it fails, it would be hard to reach. It has its own special glue designed for flexible PVC.

PVC pipe is simply cut, cleaned or primed, and glued. There are different kinds of glues for different circumstances. A good medium weight glue is recommended to withstand the chemicals and vibration that water creates flowing through the pipe. There are also glues that can handle being wet and heated up to certain degrees.

Another pipe that is used in home plumbing is CPVC. This is chlorinated polyvinyl chloride pipe. It is used for hot water and not used in pools normally. The reason that I bring this up is that some of the valves and check valves used in building pools and spas are made of this product. It requires the use of multi-purpose glue that will glue PVC, CPVC, ABS, (which is the black sewer and drain pipe) to make a good solid glued section. By using regular PVC glue on these products you can cause leaks to form, and then repair is needed. If you are ever in doubt about what kind of product was used on a particular plumbing part or part you are installing in a pool or spa, use the multi-purpose glue to prevent problems in the future.

To do plumbing and repairs is quite simple but I do have some advice for you. When you cut a piece of pipe using a saw there are pieces of debris on the outside and inside of the pipe that you cut. Simply take a pocketknife and scrape the inside and outside of the pipe. It is important to keep those little pieces from getting into places that can damage or clog up something. It is extremely important for those people who are doing their own sprinkler systems. If you do not remove those small pieces of PVC, you will spend a considerable amount of time cleaning sprinkler heads get clogged. Not fun. Remember in the introduction where I stated that my father had a golf course and country club. Well, I spent a lot of time taking apart sprinkler heads removing pieces of PVC.

After removing these particles, lightly sand the outside of the pipe that is going into the fitting or part that you are gluing. I have to admit that unless the pipe is extremely dirty and the cleaner cannot clean the dirt off, I usually do not sand the pipe. It is advisable that you sand to rough up the surface so the glue has a mechanical bond.

There are cleaners and primer for PVC pipe that are applied before gluing. When using either one, apply to the pipe and the fitting so that it works properly. It softens the PVC so the glue can have a better effect. It is like welding. In reality you are solvent-welding plastic pipe.

After you clean or prime the areas that are going to be glued, coat both the outside of the pipe and the inside of the fitting with an even coat of glue and fit them firmly to each other. Performing a slight twisting action when you connect the two pieces aids in the complete distribution of glue to all areas. You need to hold those pieces together for a few seconds so they do not slip apart. When the plumbing is glued, wait before putting liquid in the plumbing. The longer it sits to cure, the better it is. If you are gluing in cold climates you need to wait longer. Waiting overnight will ensure a good bond, and you will not have to redo the job.

Measurement of PVC is just like anything else. It depends on the size of pipe used and on the length of pipe that goes inside a fitting. Older pools were plumbed with one and a half-inch pipes, while most of the newer pools have a minimum of two-inch pipe to give better flow. A few people dry fit the pipe and fitting to make sure everything fits. I do not do that, and I must stress to you that if you dry fit fittings and pipe, make sure that you glue all that you have fitted. Too many times a pipe was dry fitted and the plumber forgot to glue the connection, and it leaked—not good if it is under a deck or pool. New installations are pressure-tested before backfilling the plumbing lines.

Another important thing to think about is backfilling. Be careful when you backfill a trench where you have installed or repaired a pipe. The pressure of fill being thrown on the pipe can crack it or damage a connection. It is not advisable to use fill that has foreign debris (such as rocks) in it. They also can crack pipe, and vibration can rub a hole in the pipe. If the trench has rocks in it, cover the pipe with a few inches of sand, and then you can use the fill that came out of the trench or hole.

Metal pipes—either galvanized or copper—are not being used anymore, or I should say it is not advisable to use them. Since the chemical process can take place if the water is corrosive, it will dissolve these metal pipes after a time. Here is an example.

I maintain a fountain located in a courtyard in the center of a home. This fountain has three lions' heads that spit water from their mouths—what I call "spitters." The home is only two years old, and the builder used copper pipe. We have to maintain proper levels of sanitizer as well as balance the pH and alkalinity because of the copper pipe. It has already turned green and the chemicals are eating the pipe away. It will not be long before a serious problem is going to arise. The copper pipe is a very thin wall pipe. Because of the release of copper off that pipe and into the water, I do not worry about algae forming in the fountain. An old time pool man told me that before algaecides were popular, he would throw 10 pennies in a trap basket of a pump and let it dissolve the copper; therefore, he made his own copper algaecide. Do not do this now because pennies are more zinc than copper, and they will cause problems. Back then, they were not worried so much about staining.

One major drawback also with metal piping is it is hard to install and repair. Galvanized pipe has to be threaded for a connection. It is almost impossible for repair applications. Copper has to be attached by soldering. It too is hard to use for repairs. PVC pipe was one of the greatest inventions ever and the best one for the pool industry. It comes with almost every imaginable fitting and coupling that needs to be used in initial plumbing and for repair.

VALVES

There are many different types of valves used on pool applications. I strongly recommend that you use a valve that is specifically made for pools. They are designed to resist corrosion of chemicals.

The worst valve that can be put on a pool system is the standard ball valve. It has a plastic handle that usually breaks and is destroyed by the chemicals. However, they are a great source of income for me and other pool professionals. I change many systems because the valves fail, and it is good money. It should be illegal for a new builder to use such a valve, but I know that most professionals in Florida use it to save money.

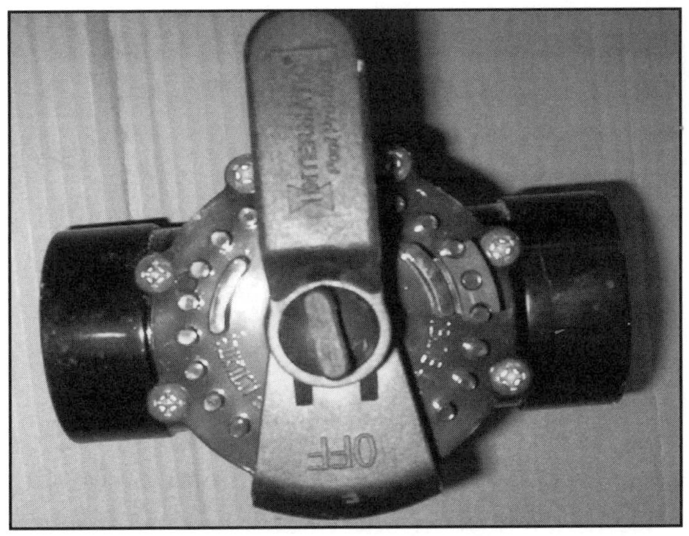

See center insert, photo twelve - standard valve.

A three-way valve has three ports. It can totally shut off the lines that are coming in and out or just shut off one or regulate them. Most new valves are self-lubricating and last for many years providing great service. The nice thing about these valves is that if the insides—get damaged, you simply take them apart and replace the worn part without cutting the valve out of the line, eliminating re-plumbing. All such valves are manual; they have to be turned manually.

I have mentioned actuators and what I refer to as an actuator valve is one that is controlled by a small electric motor. It is used with different control systems to perform different functions.

Let's say we have a system that has a spa and a pool. Normal operation means that the pool is running and the spa is overflowing into the pool. We want to use the spa in that function alone, and we push a button on the controller or the remote for the spa mode. With most systems, it shuts off the circulation pump to the pool, but not always, and electrically moves the valve from an overflow position to the spa position.

Depending on the setup, it could use one or two actuators. It opens the valve to the main drain of the spa so that it can circulate only the water in the spa with no spillover and at the same time turns on the heater to the spa. By doing this, it turns off the return lines that feed the spa in the normal mode to overflow. We will get into the different controls later but this gives you an idea what I have been talking about.

CHECK VALVES

Check valves are very simple but important devices. They simply let water flow in one direction but not in the other. They are used in situations where you do not want water to go backwards. Some use a check valve on the suction side of the pump so it does not lose its prime by siphoning the water out of the pump. This is primarily used on systems where the pool is some distance from the equipment and cuts down on the time for the pump to prime itself and flow water so the pump does not run without water present.

Most new check valves are made like valves so that they can be taken apart and have new insides installed without cutting the plumbing.

Check valves are required when a line is being shared or there are multiple pumps doing the same function. They keep the pumps from starving each other. For example, let's say that we have a pool and spa combination. The builder chose to use the suction line from the skimmer to feed the pool pump and also feed the pump that performs only the task of providing water into the spa to overflow the water for the waterfall effect. We have a three-horsepower pump circulating the pool and a one and a half-horsepower pump providing water for the overflow.

If both pumps are feeding off the same line, which one do you think will win the battle? Without a check valve, the three-horsepower pump will starve the smaller pump, affecting the initial priming of both pumps. When a pump primes in a situation like this without a check valve, the suction will go through the other pump with the least resistance.

That brings up a good point. Let's say we drained a pool or have a new pool that we are firing up for the first time. Since the water is in the skimmer and the lines, it usually takes less time to pull that water to the pump than it would if you were to try to suck all the lines together. It takes a lot of pressure to suck lines that have been dry and may have an airlock in them. The shorter and closer to the elevation of the pump, the easier it is for the pump to prime. Airlocks are rare but they can happen. By turning off all the valves except for the closest skimmer, the pump has to work less to achieve a good prime. Once it has taken off, you can slowly open the additional lines one at a time letting them clear themselves of all air before opening more lines. This is a time for patience. Take your time and watch what is going on. This is the time to spot unforeseen problems such as needing a check valve. Even if you are not going to use this particular suction line, it should be purged of air first, and you can cut it off. You will know whether there are any blockages in the lines or if you have a suction leak—extremely important when firing up a new pool.

I will not go into the old brass and galvanized gate valves. Those valves have the knob that you turn to open and close. If they have not been replaced by now, they should be.

UNIONS

A union should be used on every pump on the suction and

pressure side of the pump. In case you have to do a repair for some kind of leak, by simply turning the outside of the union you can remove the pump quickly without re-plumbing.

A union has four parts. It has two shoulders that fit up against each other with an o-ring or seal in between. It has a collar with female threads and the other shoulder has male threads that pull one shoulder tight against the other for a watertight fit. They are tightened by hand. Using a pair of channel locks will cause you to apply too much pressure, and the collar will break. I have done it many times.

AUTOMATIC WATER LEVELERS

Automatic Water Levelers are very simple devices and if installed right, they perform two functions. They add water when the level is low and remove water when the level gets too high. They use the same type of device that the old swamp coolers use in the non-humid locations of the country. They are just a water float connected to a shutoff valve so that when the level reaches a pre-set point, it shuts the water off. If the level drops below this pre-set point, it adds water. Some use a device that is like the fill valve in your toilet. Usually they just have a hole in them so that when the water level reaches that hole, water escapes keeping the level of the pool at a certain point. They can be plumbed where the water is released to a designated point.

Automatic water levelers can be a problem since they constantly try to keep a certain water level in a pool. If a pool has a small leak, it may not be detected until the leak exceeds the volume of water that is going into the pool.

CHAPTER 2

The Equipment

THE PUMP

Swimming pool pumps are manufactured by many different companies and use many different horsepower ratings that are able to move water at different rates of flow for different requirements and functions. The size of the piping and the size of the suction and pressure openings in the pump also have a great effect on gallons-per-minute flow rates.

Basic pumps consist of a housing, a motor, an impeller, and a strainer basket. They belong to the class of centrifugal pumps. A centrifugal pump impeller has a hole in the center where water enters and as the motor spins, it slings the water out through slots around the diameter of the impeller and usually inside a diffuser, which slows the action down and controls the flow. As water flows, suction or a vacuum is created and as it pulls water into the intake side of the pump, it forces water out of the pressure side of the pump. The suction pressure is referred to as head pressure. Pressure is created but because of the design of the pump, actual pressure is limited and will not continue to increase beyond a certain pressure.

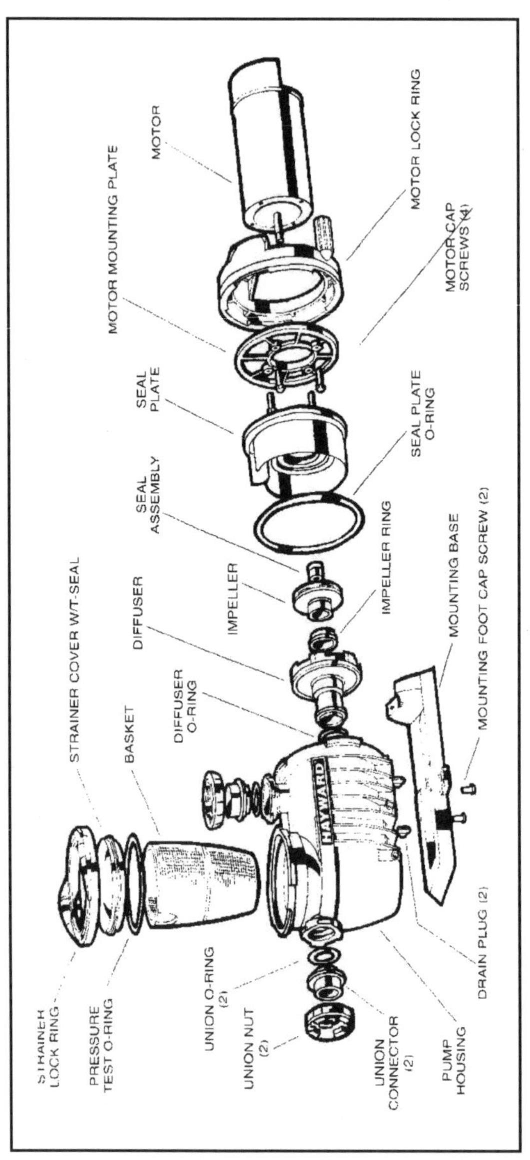

Photo courtesy of Hayward Pool Products

Through the years, pumps have been redesigned and the same items in the older pumps are different from the new, more efficient ones.

A seal, called a shaft seal, goes between the impeller and what is called a seal plate, usually made of ceramic materials. It is a two-part seal that keeps the water from escaping out of the pump. The ceramic seal is like the one used on automotive air conditioning compressors. Motors are matched up with the impellers and should not be switched. A lower rated impeller can be used on most pumps, but you do not increase the rated impeller over the horsepower of the motor. Doing so could cause the efficiency of the pump to drop and also put too much strain on the motor, resulting in premature motor failure. Whenever a motor or impeller is replaced, new seals must be used.

Common problems here in Florida are that the motors usually rust out before their time because they sit out in the open among the elements. I have seen motors run that have the whole bottom sides of the motor rusted away to where you can see the field coils, but they still run.

Now pool motors have different ratings and many have different starting and running mechanisms, but we won't get into that in this book. The main thing to remember is that if a motor goes bad and you need to replace it, use the recommended replacement motor from your supplier. Also, if you have no experience with electricity, do not touch a thing. It can kill you.

Many motors are powered by 220 volts with up to 20 amp breakers that could send you up in smoke. On any electric powered piece of equipment, always turn off the breakers to the unit and DO NOT TRUST the markings on the breaker box. Always test for power using the right test meter. Again, if you have no experience with electricity, standing in water and playing with electricity is not a smart idea, and an electrician should be called in. I am all for making or saving money, but it is not worth dying for.

Now we are going a step further. If you ever have to replace a motor, you might notice when you check the manual of specifications that the impeller on your one-horsepower motor is actually for a three-quarter horsepower pump. I know the feeling. You think you are getting shorted. This is important to understand since the pump motor is probably the most replaced piece of equipment other than the pressure gauge on the filter. Electric motors have different ratings. Each manufacturer has its own name for different ratings.

The other end of a pump is what we refer to as the wet end. That consists of the front housing and the strainer housing, which I call a trap because it traps debris that has passed through either the main drain or the skimmer basket.

Motors can come in 115 volt, 230 volt, or can be a combination where you can connect them to either. Very important here: make sure you use the correct setting on the back of the motor during replacement to prevent damage to the motor. Most pool and spa pumps are single phase. You will not see the different phases of electricity unless you get into commercial applications.

This is how this goes. A one-horsepower motor has a usable output equal to 746 watts of power. Watts are determined by multiplying the voltage by the amps. A 115-volt motor should draw 6.49 amps to produce one horsepower. Simply, the 115 volts times the 6.49 amps, equals 746 watts. These ratings that I was talking about have to do with the efficiency of the motor. If a one-horsepower motor draws more than the 6.49 amps, it is not as efficient as a motor that draws the true 6.49 amps. This has to do with the internal construction of the motor and wiring size.

Now some of the newer motors are capable of actually producing more power than they are rated. This has to do with what is called a service factor. Let us say that you have a motor with a service factor of 1.25. The 1.25 rating is per horsepower. That means it is capable of producing 1.25 horsepower even if it is rated as a one-horsepower motor. The same is true if you have a service factor of .75. That means it is not as strong as a true one-horsepower rating. That is why you will see some lower rated impellers in some pool pumps affecting the flow rates. You do not always get what you think you got. Therefore, it is important to be certain of the service rating of the motor before you install a motor, especially if the pump is critical for the flow needed to provide enough flow of water to perform a certain task. Certain pool cleaners require a certain amount of suction to operate correctly.

The service factor is a measurement of how much the motor can be overworked or overloaded before it overheats. If it is not equipped with a safety device, the motor just simply burns up or melts down. In advertisements you may see different ratings and names called fully rated or up-rated. Find the service factor on the tag on the motor or find a specification sheet that gives the actual service factor to find out the true rating of the motor. If a lower rated motor is replaced, you could have some serious circulation problems and may have some features that do not function properly. It could make for a very unhappy customer.

A properly maintained pool can extend the life of a pool pump. Chemicals out of proper range can prematurely damage a pump. Not cleaning the strainer basket in the pump can lead to failure and damage. Debris that is plugging it up can cause a low water flow and can burn up the pump and plumbing. Lack of lubrication on the strainer lid o-ring or seal can cause it to wear and rot. Many excellent silicone lubes are made for pool o-rings. Do not use a petroleum based lube on pool o-rings. It can damage an o-ring and can make it swell.

Always check for water around the pump that may indicate a leak. A leak can be serious and cause the pump not to prime and to burn up. Running a dry pump can result in so much heat that it can actually melt the strainer basket in the trap and you will have to cut it out. It usually destroys the seal in the fitting to the suction side of the pump, allowing it to suck air also and making the pump unable to create a good amount of suction to draw water from the pool to the pump.

A pump is rated by the ability to flow water through a certain size pipe. Flow is measured by gallons per minute, which has many variables including the draft or the amount in feet that it has to pull the water to the pump to the length that the pump has to push the water through the pipe. Every bend or turn of the pipe or coupling adds to the resistance of the flow of water.

The size of pipe makes a big difference. A larger size pipe reduces some of the resistance of flow. Too much pump for the size of pipe you have can prevent proper operation of the pump. Not enough water flowing to the suction side of the pump can cause cavitations (where the impeller is turning but it is just beating water). Cavitation is the formation of partial vacuums in a liquid by a swiftly moving solid body such as an impeller or propeller. It is a result of the collapse of the vacuums in a surrounding liquid. It sounds complicated. Very little flow is involved during this. If you would like to see cavitation, while the pump is running, turn off the suction line to the pump just for a couple of seconds and watch the water just move around and not flow.

FILTERS

Filtration is the most important part of a pool system in my opinion. Primarily on residential pools, there are three types of filters. They are the sand filter, the cartridge filter, and the diatomaceous earth (DE) filter. There are differences in quality of filtering and maintenance.

THE SAND FILTER

The sand filter is one of the cheapest - and the worst - kind of filter. We measure filtration in microns, which are the size of debris that can pass through the filtration system. The sand filter usually filters around 40 microns, which is very small, but the more debris that is in the filter, usually the better it filters.

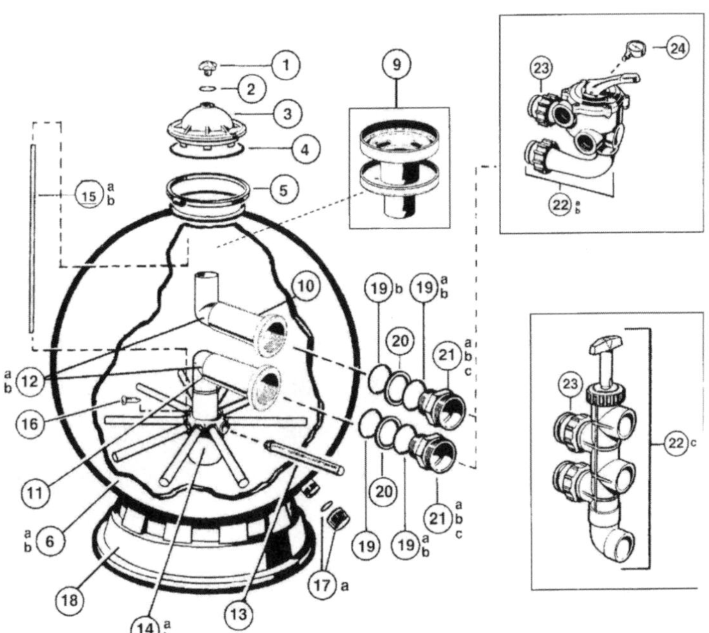

Photo courtesy of Hayward Pool Products

Expanded view of a typical sand filter

It works by water flowing through special sand that is sized for filtration, and as this water flows through the media, it cleans the water of unwanted items. Sand filters usually have a slide valve or a multiport valve for directing the water flow. Normal operation is that as the water passes through the sand, it is forced to laterals. They are multiple tubes in the bottom of the filter that go back to the top of the filter through the valve and back to the pool. To clean the filter, the valve is placed in the backwash position and the pump is turned on to reverse the flow of water through a discharge port taking the unwanted debris with it. It is a good idea to turn off the pump, put the valve back on filter, run pump for a short time, and repeat the process. You continue doing this until clear water comes out of the discharge so that when the valve is put back on filter, the pressure has dropped from the time you started. To determine that pressure has dropped, you take a reading of the initial pressure when the filter is installed or the sand is changed and mark it down or have a gauge that you can move to show the starting pressure. When the pressure reaches 10 psi above the starting pressure, it is time to backwash. If the pressure does not come down and the water is clear, then the media, or sand, is contaminated and it is time to change the sand. Make sure you use the recommended type of sand from the manufacturer. Play sand will only work in the sand box, not in the filter.

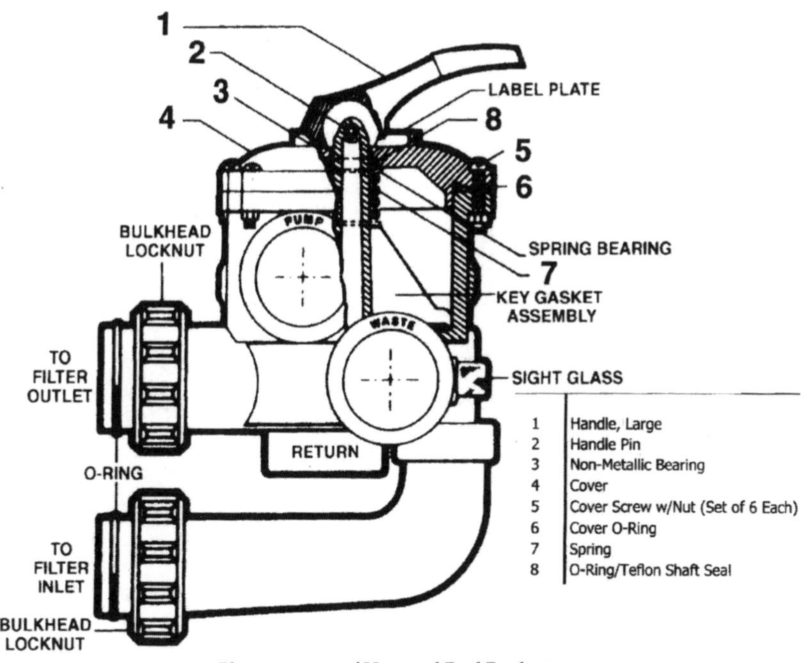

Photo courtesy of Hayward Pool Products

Breakdown of a multi-port valve

If the filter is equipped with a slide valve, it usually only has two functions: to filter and to backwash. On a multi-port valve, they have from four to six positions. They have a waste position, which bypasses the filter and disposes of the water through the discharge port. Some have rinse positions that clean the lines after backwashing so that unwanted debris will not return to the pool or filter. Some have a closed position that closes the filter. Watch this one. If you turn on the pump in the closed position, you may ruin and rupture either the filter or valve. They have the filter and backwash position, and some have what is called a boost or bypass position. This position bypasses the filter and returns it to the pool. It is used whenever a problem exists in the filter, but you still want to circulate the pool, or you have a spa and need a little extra pressure for more flow of water. ALWAYS turn off the pump whenever you are changing positions on the valve.

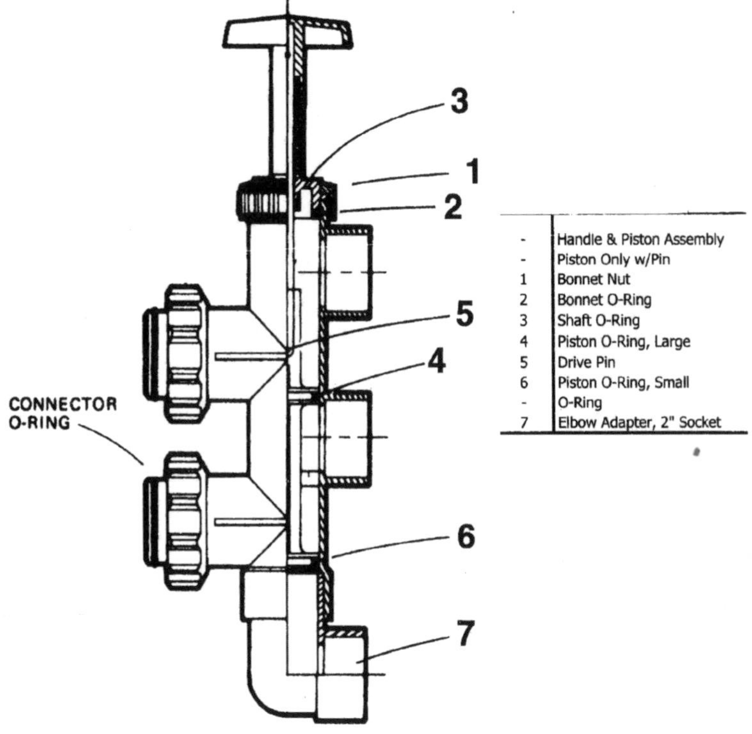

-	Handle & Piston Assembly
-	Piston Only w/Pin
1	Bonnet Nut
2	Bonnet O-Ring
3	Shaft O-Ring
4	Piston O-Ring, Large
5	Drive Pin
6	Piston O-Ring, Small
-	O-Ring
7	Elbow Adapter, 2" Socket

Photo courtesy of Hayward Pool Products

Breakdown of a typical slide valve

The waste position is useful to drain excess water out of the pool and also for getting rid of debris on the bottom of the pool that you do not want to pass through the filter. Then you can vacuum the pool to waste, and the water and debris will go from the pool directly to the discharge port and out.

Sand filters are losing their popularity, even though they are the easiest and cheapest to use. Most commercial filters are sand filters. Maintenance and the type of construction of a commercial pool is the main reason for the filter type.

CARTRIDGE FILTERS

A cartridge filter consists of a container that is usually tall and not very round depending on the size of filter. It separates a lid or top of the filter from the main base for access to the filter element. The element in a cartridge filter resembles an air cleaner on a semi truck. When cleaning is needed, you remove the element and spray it off with a high-pressure hose. You continue to spray between the folds until only clean water runs from the element. After doing that and you put the element back into the filter, if the pressure is still high or shows very little difference, further cleaning is needed. How you clean it depends on what is clogging the filter. You can spend some good money on filter cleaners and after their usual set time of 5 to 30 minutes, if you spray the element again, you have the same problem. Filters that are clogged with oils, lotions, and some basic pool products need to be soaked with a solution that contains enzymes which are available at pool supply stores, but I use Dawn or Joy dishwashing liquid   the cheap stuff. We put a half cup of dishwashing liquid into plastic trashcans and let the filters soak for two days. We take them out and spray them until no more soap comes out. I let them dry in the sun and once dried I simply pick them up. If they are light and feel right, they are clean.

If a 75-square foot filter weighs 50 pounds, you have a different problem. Then they go to another trashcan on 3:1 muriatic acid and water. If the filter contains metals or calcium, it will foam. Once the foaming stops, you can remove it and spray it off. Simply let it dry again and once dry, you just pick it up and feel the weight. If it is lighter, you have successfully cleaned a filter. If not, it may be time to replace it or use a stronger solution of acid. Most of my customers have two filters, so if I need to clean one, I have a week to clean it and return it without disrupting the functions of the pool. Cleaning an element takes time and patience.

Cartridge filters usually filter down to 20 microns, and that can be increased by adding a little diatomaceous earth to the skimmer and letting it suck up and coat the filter, or you can use a fiber-based product designed for this. They are cheap and work very well.

My main complaint about a cartridge filter is that when you vacuum the pool, much of the debris returns back to the pool since the particles of debris are smaller than the micron rating of a cartridge filter. That means that when you vacuum a pool much of the debris that you vacuum turns around and goes back in the pool. Most of this type of debris is chemical and algae by-products.

The negative factor of the cartridge filter is that you must manually remove and clean the element. It requires replacement from time to time, and they are not cheap. A cartridge filter is truly a hands-on filter. To clean it you have to touch it and not turn a valve. Sounds like manual labor, doesn't it?

THE DIATOMACEOUS EARTH (DE) FILTER

DE filters are by far the best on the market. Usually they cost more than sand or cartridge filters, but their performance is excellent. They can filter on the average down to three to seven microns. We are dealing with very small particles. It is time to get out the microscope to see anything that small. They also use a slide or a multi-port valve.

A couple of types of DE filters are a finger type with long narrow fingers that the water passes through and the newer, more efficient filter called a vertical grid filter. The DE filter works like this: a coating of DE is usually poured into the skimmer, and it sucks up in the filter and coats the grids or fingers of the filter. Debris is caught in this media and is trapped in the DE. When the pressure rises just as with the other filters, you backwash the filter. This reverses the water flow like the sand filter and washes the DE and the debris off the grids or the fingers, and passes through the valve and out the discharge port of the multi-port or slide valve. After the filter has been backwashed, you replace the proper amount of DE back in the filter and you are up and running.

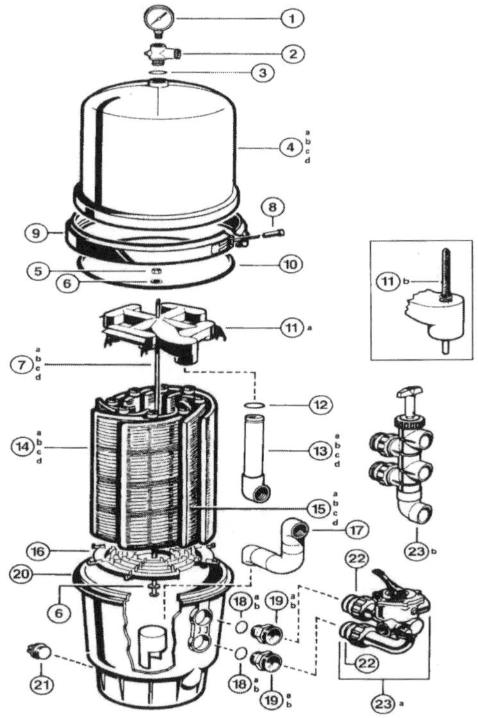

Photo courtesy of Hayward Pool Products

Breakdown of a grid DE filter

If a multi-port valve is used, they usually have fewer positions than the sand filter. Basic functions consist of filtering, backwashing, the waste position that bypass the filtration system and go out the discharge port; and the bypass or boost position, which allows for water circulation but does not go through the filter. A very important procedure to remember is that whenever you change the position of a multi-port valve you MUST turn off the pump first. Failure to do so can result in damage to the equipment and maybe even to you. The same procedure must be used if the filter is equipped with a slide valve. Refer to figures 2-1 and 2-2. for valve diagrams.

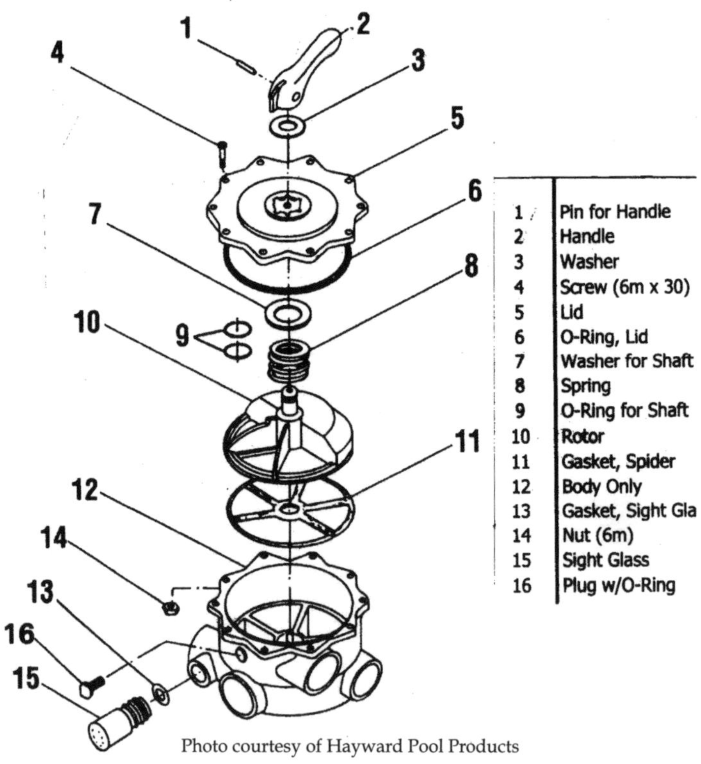

Photo courtesy of Hayward Pool Products

Figure 2-1. Breakdown of multi-port valve

A slide valve has only two features: the filtration position and the backwash position. I do not like these types of valves since you cannot drain water out of the pool without losing your DE.

The DE filter will clean a pool faster and make the water clearer than the other two types. They do require periodic cleaning but the grid filters are simple. It is a good idea to schedule cleaning at the start of every season. The "DO NOT" is to run the pool without adding the proper amount of DE because you will clog the grids and possibly damage them. A properly maintained DE filter will work well for years.

Cleaning the grids in a DE filter can be done in three ways, depending on what has clogged them. If you have treated for phosphates or have sand introduced into them that is usually from the startup of a new pool that was not cleaned properly before it was filled, you may get away with separating the upper part of the filter and simply pressure washing the grids with a hose to remove the debris. We will get into cleaning deeper in the maintenance part of the equipment.

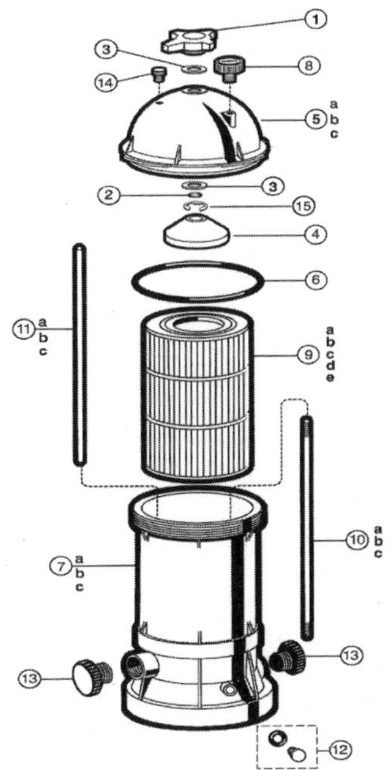

Photo courtesy of Hayward Pool Products

Figure 2-2. Break down of cartridge

HEATERS

Now unless you are using solar to heat your pool, it is expensive. Your water balance must be right, metals must be removed, and due to the abuse of a pool heater, they can be expensive to use and maintain. I will not write in detail about heating, since you must have more than a pool-cleaning license to work on them. Most are propane or natural gas, although wood-fired pool heaters and some electric heaters are still being used. Wood heating a pool seems to be on the rise in the Northern States due to some new products. Spa heaters are usually electric if they are portable or small. Heating water also causes certain problems maintaining water balance. We will dive into that in the chemistry section of the spas. In the northern states, fuel oil heaters are still being used. There are still a few fuel oil heater manufacturers in the United States.

If you have a customer who wants to add a heater to his or her pool and you have no knowledge of heating a pool and the equipment, call an expert. Improper size of the heater, poor plumbing, and a few other factors can make it costly and inefficient to use. Also, since most states require certification and licensing for a qualified heating professional, you should not do it. If you plumb the heater, make sure you get your flow rates right. Improper flow through a heat exchanger can result in ruining the efficient operation of the design and performance of the unit itself. It can also cost your customer a great deal of money if it is not working properly.

Spas are a different story, and we will get into that in the spa section.

TIMERS

Timers or time clocks are used on most pools. They may be the very simple time clock that you set or they can be sophisticated electronic timers that can perform multiple tasks and even produce chlorine for the pool or spa in pre-adjusted parts per million. These systems will be discussed in Chapter 13.

Timers can be incorporated with other functions and can come in the standard clock model or in the electronic timer that can deal with many different modes and pieces of equipment. Some still have the pressure switch that has a plunger that pushes air through a hose and forces another plunger to turn a switch on in the control. Some of these timers can do up to four different functions. They are very safe since the electrical part of the spa is located away from the water, reducing the chance of someone being electrocuted.

LIGHTING

Pool and spa lighting varies from pool to pool and spa to spa. It can be a simple light or go to the extreme with fiber optic lighting that can produce many different looks and options. I have seen some pools that remind me of a fireworks display with dancing light on water.

Pool lights can have low voltage of 12 volts to a high of 120 volts. The fiber optic lighting system produces light with no power located at the light. It has a stationary box that produces lighting, usually in different colors. This light flows through the fiber optics cable and can be designed and installed almost anywhere along a pool or spa. Fiber optic lighting is limited only to the imagination of the installer. I have no vision of colors or design of artistic things. I leave the lighting installation to the people who specialize in that field. Currently there are many different manufacturers of fiber optic lighting.

When replacing a bulb in a pool or spa remember to turn off the power, test to make sure power is off, and do not get water in the light fixture itself. Most have a protective measure so that when moisture is detected, it will not work and will blow the GFI breaker.

If you have to pull a new light in a pool or spa, remember that water will be in the conduit with the wire up to the water level. No splices are allowed. Lights come with different lengths of cable so you can purchase the one closest to the length that you need. Most codes for construction have an amount of wire that must be left in the niche in order to remove the light assembly and lift above the water line. Preferably, you will be able to set the light on the deck for easy replacement. If this has not been done, remove the proper amount of water to lower it below the light level. When you replace the light assembly, leave the proper amount of cable so it can be serviced later. Usually you can remove a light without getting into a pool, depending on where the light was installed and to what depth. Normal distance between the level of water and the light is 18 to 24 inches. With the new pool designs some may be deeper or under a water feature.

Let's stray for a minute and imagine a hot, humid day. The nice thing about this business is that you can always find a reason to get into the pool. You might need to perform safety check on the drain covers. This is not only a good excuse but it is also a vital check to ensure that the covers are properly secured so no one can be hung up in a drain. Inspection of the mounting of a light is also a good reason. Being out in the sun all day working on pools really can dehydrate you, and it can be dangerous while working with chemicals.

If you feel the need to cool down in a hurry, just jump in or take your shoes off and soak your feet. The numerous blood vessels in your feet act like a radiator in a car and can cool your body off. Make sure you drink plenty of liquids. Do not sacrifice your personal safety and health by being in a hurry to make money. Here is the second rule. Do not have your cell phone on your body while working on pools. I have not found a true water-proof cell phone yet. My service provider loves me. He knows that he will sell a couple of new phones to me every year.

SELF-CLEANING SYSTEMS

A self-cleaning system sounds like a conflict of interest. There is no such monster as a self-cleaning pool. I have seen some that come close, but they are not totally self-cleaning.

These systems I call the "pop-ups" or the "Caretaker" system. The Caretaker is a brand of system that has swimming pool floor fittings with a removable rotating valve that rises when water pressure is applied to it and forces the head up directing water flow to a certain position in the pool. When the flow of water is shut off to the pop-up, it retracts, but because of the design, it rotates a few degrees. Each time the pop-up comes up and down, it rotates a certain degree. These pop-ups are plumbed in zones.

The way they should work is to start in one spot and force the debris towards the deep end of the pool where the drain is located. They do not clean the pool but direct the debris to the drain where it can remove it and send it to the filter for removal. If installed properly, they work very well not as good as a good old vacuuming but effective. The pop-up system was designed to limit the maintenance that a homeowner has to perform.

The pop-up system is controlled by a diverter that changes the zones on a pre-program. Different companies manufacture these self-cleaners. Sometimes the maintenance on these systems is expensive to maintain and needs regular maintenance. You need to weigh the need and advantages and the initial cost and maintenance of any system to see if it is right for you.

In the first paragraph of this section I said that there was no such monster as the self-cleaning pool, but pool owners have been told that this is exactly what this system does, and they are the unhappy ones. Make sure whether it is a simple equipment change or a sophisticated system you explain the system very well to customers and let them decide if they need it. Promising things in this business will have negative repercussions. There are too many variables.

CHAPTER 3

Water Chemistry

BASIC WATER ANALYSIS

Water testing is a simple procedure that everyone including the pool owner needs to perform at regular intervals. Over-testing in not necessary since it takes time to change water and make it respond. Unlike in a spa, the addition of chemicals to a pool will take time to mix with the water. The preferred outcome of pool circulation is that a pool circulates the amount of gallons of water that it has in it per day or per cycle. That is where the builder will either build a successful, low maintenance pool or make a demon that will drive you crazy trying to get it to respond.

Balanced water is non-corrosive and non-irritating. Water, in an unbalanced form can damage equipment and your pool and make it very unpleasant for the swimmer. When water is corrosive, it can become very aggressive and can dissolve concrete and metals. Pool water that is out of balance can eat the metal inside a heat exchanger of a heater creating a very expensive repair and a very unhappy pool owner. It can pit the surface of a pool. Staining can occur and on a new pool can void the warranty of the surface and equipment.

To get a sample of water to test, I use a bottle that I purchased from a chemical supplier so that when you fill it and put the lid back on, it has a straw-like pipe that sticks out of the lid. When you squeeze the bottle, a controlled amount of water comes out and you can accurately put the proper level of water in each test vial—extremely important. The wrong water level in the test vial will create incorrect readings. Also, most bottles of reagents work more accurately if you hold the bottle straight up and down instead of angled. You take the water sample away from a pool return and try to get the sample approximately 18 inches below the water line. Being near a return can give you false levels, especially if you have a pool with a chlorine generator. It is best if the pool has circulated for a time before the sample is taken. Better to stir it all up together to get an accurate reading. ALWAYS test your water before the addition of any chemicals.

The procedure that I use is that my crew tests for sanitizer level, pH, and alkalinity on a weekly basis. We test for stabilizer and calcium hardness on a monthly basis, since they change slower than the other factors. Certain other tests are done depending on the area, known source water problems, and by visual inspection of the pool and equipment.

The task of the professional or owner is a very simple one. Keep the water balanced to avoid any problems and unnecessary repairs. Parameters are set that determine the balance of the water. This section will go into the testing of the sanitizer, pH, total alkalinity, calcium hardness, and total dissolved solids (TDS).

This is one of the most interesting and controversial areas that you will ever see. Everyone in the pool business and anyone who has ever had a pool, including those weekend kiddy pools, seems to be an expert in water chemistry. As I said before, every pool and spa has its own characteristics and no two are the same. I am attempting to introduce you to the basic tests and adjustments. It is up to you to fine tune your pool for the best performance. You have to remember that you will be dealing with Mother Nature, and she can be a very powerful influence on your water's staying balanced. Do not believe everything that someone other than a professional tells you, and you might be a little skeptical of some of them, too. If you are having a particular problem with your pool, and your neighbor or friend is having a similar problem, you may have different reasons for these problems. Each situation is different and calls for different approaches.

Sanitizers are not part of the basic balancing of water, but they do affect the testing, and each chemical has its own characteristics, interactions, and side effects. Remember that each sanitizer has a different pH level, which will affect the balance. We will get to that in the chapter on chemicals.

HYDROGEN POWER (pH)

A standard that the beer industry came up with back in the early 1900s, it stood for potens hydrogen, Latin for hydrogen power. This is the measurement of acidity that is caused by the hydrogen ion.

A pH scale runs from 0-14 with a pH reading of seven considered neutral. If under seven, it is considered acidic, and above seven it is considered basic or alkaline. To give you an example that Taylor Technologies describes, the pH scale is logarithmic which means that every whole unit increase is 10 times it predecessor. What this means is that if you have a pH of six, it is ten times more acidic that a pH of seven and a pH of three is 10,000 times more acidic than a PH of seven. That shows you how important the control of pH in a pool or spa is. Pool water is kept slightly alkaline and the recommended parameters are for a range of 7.2 to 7.8 with the ideal at 7.4 to 7.6. One thing to remember is that if you have low pH and chlorine is introduced into the water, it can be very corrosive. If a pool or spa is using bromine as a sanitizing agent, it is more critical. Bromine is very aggressive and can dissolve metals quickly. The old standard that I have always gone by is that when you have a chlorine reading of 7.2 your chlorine works at 80 percent. At 7.8 it works at 20 percent. Keeping your pH in the lower range can improve the effectiveness of the sanitizer, but you have to be aware that it is more corrosive if the levels get too low. There is more on this in Chapter 5.

Even though this is the first test that I have introduced, it is not the first that you adjust. You lower the pH level with acid, which comes in various forms discussed later, and you raise pH with soda ash, or in some cases, you may have to use sodium bicarbonate.

You will see this several times. NEVER, NEVER, mix any form of acid with any other chemical that you use, and ALWAYS pour acid into water, and NEVER pour water into acid. Chemical reactions can occur by ignoring absolute safety with chemicals. Always refer to the product safety labels and MSD sheets.

Once a chemical is added to adjust the pH factor of your water, it has to mix and stabilize before you can get an accurate reading. Some say four hours, but the water needs to circulate totally and mix well. At least give it a day, and then if it is questionable, give it another. This is all dependent on how well the equipment was designed and if it is functioning properly. If the pool is functioning properly and I add acid to a pool, I always restrict the use of the pool for four hours. This allows the chemicals to be dispersed so there are no problems. Safety is the key here.

Problems that occur with low pH are concrete pitting, metals dissolving, staining of walls, and losing chlorine. In vinyl pools, the liner can wrinkle and bathers can have skin and eye irritations. When the pH is high, the problems can be scaling of lines and the pool walls. Chlorine inefficiency can also cause skin and eye irritations.

TOTAL ALKALINITY

Alkalinity can best be described as "buffer." Total alkalinity is the measurement of the ability of your water to resist wild and sudden changes in pH. These sudden changes are called "spiking."

Since every chemical you add to your pool has different pH factors, the total alkalinity is very important to keep sudden fluctuations down and decrease the chance of spiking. This is one of the main reasons that you always adjust your alkalinity before you adjust your pH. Remember that. Alkalinity before pH.

The alkalinity level in your pool helps with many things. Some say that it helps prevent algae. I know of some old timers who claim that they raise alkalinity whenever they have an algae problem. I lower the pH to get the best bang out of my buck for the chlorine. Until the pool is clear, the alkalinity reading is not really important unless it is totally unbalanced.

Low alkalinity can result in corrosive water that can damage heaters, and if it is down for a long enough time, it can pit concrete and your pool surface. It can dissolve metals and stain walls. Too high alkalinity scales water, which in turn can cloud your water and reduce circulation. Also, when your alkalinity levels are low, pH levels bounce, which is rapid spiking and fluctuations of pH. High alkalinity readings usually cause the pH to drift upward.

The recommended levels for alkalinity under the 2005 ANSI/NSPI Guidelines for chemical parameters is 60 to 180. I prefer the old recommendations of 80 to 150, with the preferred of 80 to 100 using calcium hypochlorite and using sodium hypochlorite as a sanitizer, and 100 to 120 using the other sanitizers in the chlorine family.

In testing of all areas if one level—such as your chlorine level in your pool—is extreme, interference can be the cause of giving you a false reading. Using the Taylor reagents, the alkalinity is a more sensitive test when testing for total alkalinity. If an interference is apparent by the discoloration of the test water, you can simply retest and add an additional drop or two of the first reagent, thiosulfate, which neutralizes chlorine. Never take a test reading after adding chemicals. Always test the water first before any additions are made. The addition of other chemicals with their own characteristics can give you the wrong readings.

CALCIUM HARDNESS

Hardness readings of pool and spa water are different from readings for drinking water. We focus on the calcium level in pool and spa water and on magnesium in drinking water. Magnesium does not scale, so it is left out of our industry primarily. If none or little of these items is present in water, we call it "soft" water, which is not desirable for pool water. Many homes have water softeners that are not plumbed separately from the faucet used for the pool, so that calcium chloride is added to arrive at the proper recommended level.

Hardness levels can sometimes be misread when levels of certain iron and copper are present in the water. There are ways to correct the interference they cause, depending on which test kit you use.

Low calcium can cause etching of the plaster on your pool, pitting of the concrete, dissolving grout used on your tile surface, and pitting of some pool decks. High calcium can plug lines from scale buildup, which can result in poor circulation, cloudy water, and a ruined pool heater. Scaling on the pool surfaces can be so severe that even acid washing a pool will not remove them. More on that later.

Proper levels recommended by the ANSI/NSPI are between 150 to 1,000 for pools and 100 to 800 for spas. The ideal levels are 200 to 400 for pools and 150 to 250 for spas. I can guarantee you that in a pool with a calcium level of 600, some serious scaling is happening, even if you cannot see it. I prefer a level of 250 for a concrete pool. Since our source water here in Florida averages about 250 to 280 for most places, we do not even carry calcium chloride on our trucks. We are in the business of balancing water, not selling chemicals. For those of you who use what is called the Langlier Index, you might disagree with me on this, but we will address the subject again later.

Unfortunately, when the calcium level gets too high, the only way to remove it is to drain and put some fresh water in. I cannot tell you how much to drain, but depending on the levels of calcium in your source water, more is better. Like us, if your source water is under 300 and your pool water is over 600, draining more water is better than draining too little. It is hard to tell an owner that you drained and refilled his or her pool and did not get enough out and have to do it again: one of those things that experience and time will help you arrive at the best answer.

CYANURIC ACID

Now this is a highly controversial area. You have to remember that most chemicals that you use are poison, and this is one to be careful with. It too, like high calcium levels, requires draining. And it is important to drain the most that you can before filling. I recently drained a 21,000 gallon pool that went from a three-foot shallow area to an eight-foot deep end. I drained the pool to where the water level was even to the center of the length of the pool on the surface. That left about three to four feet just in the deep end. Its readings were off my test kit that goes up to 100 ppm. After I filled the pool, I let the water circulate for a day, came back, and tested. I had a reading of a good 50 ppm.

This is where I differ with many people of the industry. The recommended levels by the ANSI/NSPI for cyanuric acid, or stabilizer as it is commonly called, is 0 to 150. A chlorine pool requires stabilization where a bromine pool does not. On a pool that uses tablets from trichlor, I like to keep the levels under 50. On a salt pool, some recommend a minimum of 80 ppm. I have done much investigation about levels of cyanuric acid in pools and the effects it has on the human body. Some areas ban the use of cyanuric acid altogether. Some local codes limit it to 100 ppm.

Some Internet reports say it is toxic and give detailed information, and some do not give you much information at all. All I can tell you is what I have observed over the years. When you get to the 100-ppm level, you will notice a significant decrease in the ability of the chlorine to sanitize. The effects that have been reported to me are an increase of ear infections in children. Eye irritation is common with high levels of cyanuric acid. Older folks have reported rashes around the genital areas, and animals that drink out of the pool suffer diarrhea. In each case, when the levels of cyanuric acid were decreased by draining and refilling the pool, these symptoms left. That's something to think about.

Cyanuric acid, CYA, or stabilizer as it is commonly called, has one purpose in the pool. It slows the decomposition of chlorine from the sun, giving chlorine a longer life. Professionals do agree that more than 100 ppm absolutely serves no purpose except to cause problems. Therefore, indoor pools do not need stabilizer.

As previously stated the only way to get rid of stabilizer is to drain and refill the pool. Stabilizer comes in various forms. A common trichlor tablet is half stabilizer. So let's say that your pool goes through six eight-ounce tablets a week. That is 24 ounces of stabilizer that you are adding to your pool every week, slowing your chemicals down and making your sanitizer ineffective. Whenever I go out to a pool that has had a problem for a long time and the pool stores cannot correct the problem even with the hundreds of dollars of chemicals they have sold this poor pool owner, I test the cyanuric level first. If it is around 90 ppm or above, all is stopped. Knowing that the chemical process is slowed to a crawl and that numerous other poisons or chemicals have been added to fix an unfixable pool, I believe it is time to get the water out of the pool. I can correct what I know, but I cannot correct excessive amounts of different chemicals that a pool owner might have added out of desperation. A good point to make is that if a label says to add eight ounces to 10,000 gallons of water, it does not mean to add more. If some works, more does not help. Certain products you put in excess into a pool can do serious damage, adding poison to the water you swim in and sometimes ingest.

For the pool owner. If you run into a problem, do not count on your average pool supply chain to help you. If you notice, most of the people in the store have no experience with pool water. Chemicals that are sold in these places normally are not of the strength that your professional can get. Discount places are the worst places to buy chemicals. Ask around and find a good pool person as ask for their help. Doing so will usually save you money in the long run and could save you thousands of dollars on repairs to your pool and equipment. If you can't find one, give me a call. I will help you.

This is a very important part. **DO NOT EVER ADD** anything to cyanuric acid. The addition of acid to cyanuric acid can be fatal. More on that later.

TOTAL DISSOLVED SOLIDS (TDS)

Now just about everything that you add to your pool has some sort of mineral residue left in your water, and it is saturated sometimes with, well, junk. Let us say you boil a pan of water on the stove until the water is all gone. What is left on the bottom of the pan is the residue from the minerals that are in your water. That is TDS. It is suspended matter in the water that is usually too small for your filtration unit to take out. Pool water becomes more corrosive as the TDS level increase.

When the water in your pool evaporates, particles stay behind.

Between that, the chemicals that you add, the lotions you use, the fine dirt that you bring in, and yes, the dog that swims once a day, the TDS mounts up in your pool.

Different sanitizers affect TDS, especially in salt pools. Most TDS is not harmful, but it can absorb your chemicals. TDS is not a thing that your pool store will test for. Most will not have test equipment to test for TDS.

Here in Florida, our TDS figures are high. Since we do not freeze, we do not drain a portion of our water every year to prevent damage from freezing. The yearly draining of an amount of water helps in the removal of TDS and lowers cyanuric acid levels. With the introduction of so many salt generating systems to produce chlorine, the salt makes the TDS go up.

I have to be honest with you. I rarely test for TDS. In my experience, when TDS gets out of hand, there is something else going wrong in the pool and it is time to change some water. I know that if I have a pool that gets a lot of calcium hypochoride added to it, there are going to be more TDS. Every 60-pound bag of salt I add to the pool is TDS. When the levels are within a good range but problems still continue, a test for TDS is required. If we changed water in all the pools that have a high TDS reading here, we would run out of water. Not to make light of this, but in some areas, you have to compensate a little. If your professional or store can test for TDS, ask for it. It can show you what is going on.

In a spa we don't worry about TDS. Since usually most portable spas are under 600 gallons, we change the water in them frequently. Lotions and ammonia from the body ruin the water in a spa fairly quickly, so you have to change it. More on this later also.

ADVANCED TESTING

IRON

I call it advanced testing, but it is still water testing for special things. Have you ever noticed a pool in which returns and drain cover have a reddish brown color? This is a perfect place to test for iron.

Iron can change the color of a surface, especially on the walls. If iron or other minerals are in your water, a chelating agent will keep the minerals in solution. A sequestering agent in some cases can remove the minerals from the surface and put them in solution so that the filter can remove them.

COPPER

Green, blue-green, or turquoise water can be pretty, but it is usually a sign of copper in the water. Copper can ruin a pool surface. I will explain this further on.

PHOSPHATES

To get to the point, phosphates are nothing more than fertilizers for algae. Pools that have a continual problem with algae should be tested and treated. Once removal is accomplished, that pool should go on a regular treatment for phosphates. You will find that getting rid of the phosphates in your pool will eliminate most of your algae problems.

Phosphates come in many forms and sources such as fertilizers, organic debris including leaves and bark, and some pool chemicals. Phosphates come from rainwater, rocks, landscaping, potted plants around your pool, swimwear and clothes washed in products containing phosphate, and cleaning solutions that contain trisodium phosphate.

Good rule of thumb: do not wash your swimwear that you use in your pool. After leaving the pool, rinse off at your outside shower or hose, and let it air dry, eliminating the problem with your laundry detergent. Make sure you keep your lawn man at a distance when he fertilizes your yard. Do not go from the ocean to your pool without rinsing yourself and your clothes first. If you live on a lake or by a river and your dog visits the lake and then likes to cool off in the pool, he could be getting even with you for something. Phosphates are in bodies of water, and animals can cross-contaminate your pool by going from a body of water with algae and then into your pool. Buy Fido a kiddy pool and keep him out of yours. It is always a good idea to take a shower or a good rinsing before entering your pool. Prevention is a lot easier than elimination.

Phosphates introduced into a pool that has a chlorine generator can eat up the chlorine and cause the production of chlorine to halt. Removal of the phosphates and some nitrates will correct this problem. Many people have paid a technician to come and repair their salt generators to find out that it was only phosphates, which are cheaper to remove than to pay for a service call. We charge $65 an hour including driving for a service call, and the average pool can be treated for a third of that. When we talk about recommended parameters for balanced water there are different guidelines depending on which organization that you use and also none supersedes the product label directions or local and state codes and regulations. This chart comes from the ANSI/NSPI (International Aquatic Foundation) guidelines for chemical operational parameters.

If you really want to fine tune your water then depending on your sanitizer, there are some different parameters for alkalinity and some spa guidelines are different.

What	Min.	Ideal	Max.	For what
Free chlorine, ppm	1.0	2.0 – 4.0	4.0 US EPA max	Residential and public pools
	2.0	3.0 – 4.0	US EPA max	Public and residential spas
Combined chlorine	0	0	0.2	All except public spas
Total bromine	1.0	2.0 – 3.0 Residential 2.0 – 6.0 Public	5.0	Public and residential pools
PHMB	30	30 – 50	50	All facilities
PH	7.2	7.4 – 7.6	7.8	All facilities
Total alkalinity	60	80 – 120	180	All facilities
TDS	NA	NA	1500 ppm over start-up TDS	All facilities
Calcium hardness	150	200 – 400	1000	All pools and aquatic facilities
	100	150 – 250	800	All spas
Cyanuric acid	10	30 – 50	150	All facilities
Ozone			0.1 over 8-hr time-wtd. avg.	All facilities

For total alkalinity, the 80-100 guideline is for the use of calcium hypochlorite, lithium hypochlorite, or sodium hypochlorite.

For total alkalinity of 100-120 guideline is for dichlor, trichlor, chlorine gas, or bromine.

Salt pools should have the low reading of 80-100 for total alkalinity.

CHAPTER 4

Cleaning The Pool

TOOLS OF THE TRADE

To do a proper pool cleaning, you need the proper equipment. The list is not limited to these items, but they are a basic requirement for an individual to do a good cleaning and take care of a pool properly.

BUCKET: This may seem to be a strange tool but it will be one thing you will use most—for mixing and diluting chemicals, removing debris from the skimmers and nets that you do not leave on the deck, carrying chemicals that do not need to drip on the pool deck, and chasing down the road when it falls off your pick-up.

The bucket can be used to acid wash equipment and to soak filters and grids. The things that you can use an empty bucket for are endless. I use empty buckets that have lids to store plumbing fittings— different o-rings and seals that are left over, as well as extra parts. They are good for hauling things to a pool such as chemicals and tools.

A bucket is used to dilute the chemicals before they are put into the water. Granular sanitizers, acids, soda ash, sodium bicarbonate, and calcium are great candidates that need to be diluted before being put into a pool or spa so that no damage is done to the surfaces, and it aids in getting the chemical into solution. You can throw a certain product into a pool and it simply falls to the floor of the pool rather than dissolving.

CORNER BRUSH: A small round brush that measures about four to six inches in diameter and fits on your pool pole, gets to those hard to reach places such as steps, corners, and other areas where the regular brush cannot reach. The areas where one uses a corner brush are usually the places where problems first appear. Use of this brush will help prevent yellow (mustard) and black algae in pools. Lack of proper brushing provides perfect places to be attacked with algae. Prevention is easier than removal.

POOL POLE: Some call it a tele-pole since it extends to certain lengths. You attach your equipment to it, such as a leaf rake, vacuum head, or brush. Most are made of lightweight materials but the best ones are fiberglass. They usually come with either an external cam lock or an internal cam lock.

Most are 8′ that extend to 16′. Some are 4′ that extend to 12′. Longer poles are made for larger residential and commercial pools. For professional use, you want the strongest pole that you can get. This is the tool that is used multiple times every day and is heavily abused.

An internal cam is my standard vacuum along with a cleaning pole that has the lock for the pole inside. It can be operated with one hand when you get the routine down. When I am skimming a pool, it allows me to lengthen the pole easily to extend to those leaves that run from me. The external cam is stronger, and I use it for heavy vacuuming and when I use my Hammerhead.

All models of poles come with two sets of holes at the working end of the pole. These are designed to attach pool tools onto the pole. Since I have no tools that attach to the upper set of holes, when they are damaged or worn out I can cut the pole off to make the tools fit into new holes.

When poles wear out, do not throw them away. Multiple poles can be attached together with screws to make a long pole for a special pool, or they can be cut off to use in fountains and spas.

POOL HOSE: Pool hoses attach from the pool vacuum to the fitting in either the cleaner port or skimmer. They come in different lengths and a couple of different diameters. Most common is the one and half inch hose. The longer the pool hose, the more restriction it has to vacuum. If your vacuum head is not equipped with a swivel, you need one on the tool end of your hose to keep the hose from coiling up.

The ends of the hose are called cuffs. They are replaceable on most hoses so when one wears out, and they will, you do not have to purchase a new hose. Professionals should use a commercial hose because of the wear that the hose suffers. The initial cost may be more, but chemicals can damage a standard pool hose and a better hose will save you money in the long run.

I have a 50′ hose that I cut to 35′. I installed new cuffs on the ends and if I need more than 35′ I add a hose connector that allows me to combine both hoses for a 50′ length. It is difficult to vacuum a 24′ pool with a 50′ hose: it just gets in the way.

LEAF EATER: This is a tool that connects to a water hose that has a bag attached to the top that comes in several different meshes (microns) that removes leaves and debris from the pool by the water creating a vacuum, sucking the debris into the bag for removal.

It sprays water in an upward direction through the throat or venturi that creates suction that works very well if the water pressure is good. It can remove a lot of debris in a short time, and the particles that are too small for the bag to catch simply pass through the bag for the filter to take out of solution.

When you are using one, it is important to secure the bag very well on the top of the cleaner. A bag that is not properly secured can come off and all the debris that was trapped in the bag will be lost back to the bottom of the pool. That is really aggravating.

There are two main designs. The concrete model has wheels, and the other model has a brush that is located around the bottom edge of the cleaner. The brush model is for a vinyl and fiberglass pool. The better models are weighted so that they will not float. Usually they attempt to rise in the water when you are pulling them back toward you. They are a useful tool for pools that get leaves in them.

Parts are replaceable on these, such as the rim—if removable—that the bag secures to, the wheel assemblies, and the handle that attaches to the pool pole. On the brush models, the brushes are also replaceable.

LEAF SKIMMER: A shallow net designed to skim the surface of the water for floating debris. I personally do not like them because I always drop more back into the pool than I get into the net.

LEAF RAKE: A frame surrounded by a deep netting to let you either skim the top of a pool for the removal of debris such as leaves, and to remove leaves and stems and lots of other things from the bottom of a pool. Some finer materials are used on some nets to trap smaller particles.

A good leaf rake has a beveled edge on the front of the rake. With it you can skim the floor of the pool, and leaves and debris will roll into the net for easy removal. Rakes are made of different materials and the costliest last the longest. It sometimes makes the removal of a few leaves easier than vacuuming the leaves up. It is also the perfect tool for removing toys that children leave in the pool. Getting a toy or object stuck in your vacuum is an aggravating situation. Those items that actually are picked up through the vacuum can be stuck in a line, and then you have big trouble.

Leaf rakes also come in a very fine mesh fabric for removing the smallest particles and bugs. The micron rating of the rake is smaller than that of a normal leaf rake and is used a great deal in spas.

SPA VACUUM: A small handheld suction device that pulls debris from spas and small areas usually by pulling on a handle. It is a very useful tool for decorative waterfalls and spillovers.

Some use a water hose like the leaf eater but on a smaller scale. It sucks the debris through a venturi-like hole in the center of the tool by forcing water in an upward direction causing the debris to go into a fine mesh bag. They work very well. The small head can get into small places and can get into weird areas of custom pools that a regular vacuum cannot get to.

TEST KITS: A test kit that is designed to test water in a pool. Some are very basic and only test for chlorine and pH, and some go deeper in testing other requirements. The best type of test kit is recommended for even the pool owner.

A good test kit will test for free and total chlorine and bromine, pH, alkalinity, calcium hardness, and stabilizer levels. Test kits also will test for many other things such as copper, iron, phosphates, biguanide, hydrogen peroxide, nitrates, acidity, chlorides (salt), ozone, manganese, and poly-quat algaecides. Some are test strip tests that are specialized for one specific item.

Test kits come in liquid, strip, powder, and tablet form. Some are more resistant to high levels of certain chemicals that can cause an interference giving you incorrect readings or wrong colors of the reagents' reactions.

TILE BRUSH: A brush that helps release oils, lotions, and debris that collect on the tile, it is used for the removal of calcium buildup on the tiles. Some are handheld, and others have an extension pole on them with a swivel head to get into those tough places—a must for all pool professionals.

TILE CLEANER: A soap that is specially designed for cleaning tiles. Some contain acid and some are made for adding acid if needed for those stubborn deposits. Tile soaps are specially formulated for fiberglass and vinyl pools. Care must be taken so that you use the right tile soap for the right pool. Since fiberglass and liner pools have no tile, they are designed to clean the waterline where the debris settles on the walls of the pool.

A very important fact about tile cleaners is that some can damage marble and grout. Be sure to follow the cautions as to what the product is designed for. Acid products can damage painted decks when the product drips off the tile brush onto the deck. If you are using such a cleaner it is recommended that you put the brush into a bucket to remove it from the pool area so that this does not happen. Acid products will also damage other things. Use caution.

WALL BRUSH: Made of a combination of things, the majority has nylon bristles, and some are a combination of nylon and stainless steel. The stainless steel brush is used for stubborn stains and algae. Brushes that have stainless steel in them should only be used on concrete pools. Do not use on fiberglass or liner pools.

A brush that is coming apart should not be used. Nylon brushes that have bristles that fall out can get into impellers of the pump and cause problems. They can force themselves in between the ceramic seals in the pump. A stainless steel brush that has bristles coming off can stain a pool and damage the cartridge and DE filters media. The bristles also hurt when one sticks in your foot. Usually rusted, they can cause infection and can result in your getting a tetanus shot.

VACUUM HEAD: Tool that is used to vacuum the bottom of your pool. The model for concrete has wheels, and the vinyl model just has a brush on the edges of the surface so it will not damage the liner.

Concrete models come in many different types of materials and strengths. Some have height-adjustable wheels and most of them flex for rounded edges. Better models have ball bearings in the wheel, and some use plastic axels. Some are wider for different applications and larger pools. The cheaper ones have the tendency to collapse if you put a good suction on and then stick them to the surface of the pool. This is where you will find out how good your pool pole is. Too much pressure used trying to get them unstuck will bend a cheap pole. If the vacuum head is stuck, it is always better to pull than to push.

The vinyl models are for vinyl pools and recommended for fiberglass pools but are also used for new surfaces of concrete so that damage will not occur. They work well on sand that has fallen in the pool during installation or during the home's construction. A model that is heavy or that is weighted works best so that it does not float. You will have to try to hold lightweight models down on the surface of the pool while vacuuming.

WATER HOSE: Use for filling pools and spas and for cleaning decks. Everyone needs one to clean filters and in some cases wash the decks off that have debris on them. A long hose with a good spray nozzle is a good item that will be used very much.

DE CUP: A cup that holds exactly one pound of DE. Other commonly used products such as Cal Hypo, cyanuric acid, soda ash, brominating tablets, and bi-carb weigh four pounds.

PUMP WRENCH: A tool that is used for the removal of lids on pumps.

CLEANING THE POOL

The procedure to clean a pool varies from person to person and from pool to pool. I will go through my recommendation for cleaning a pool that is mildly dirty and without algae. We will tackle the extremely dirty pools later in the chapter.

The first thing that should be done is a basic walk around so that you see leaks and check on whether the equipment is performing properly. A check of the pressure gauge will let you know two things: whether you will have to clean the filter and whether you need to look at the adjustments and settings of the valves that might limit the performance of the system. The best tools I use are my ears. I can tell many things by the sound of a pump running.

Let us start with the pressure gauge. Let's say that we have a system that has been running at an average of 16 psi. We know that as the filter traps more debris and starts to get plugged the pressure rises. If it is at 26 psi we know that it is time to clean the filter or to backwash it depending on what kind of filter it is. This system on this day is at 6 psi.

What that should tell you is that either you have a bad gauge or you have a problem. Look at the pool to see if water is flowing with the same vigor that it always does. If the pool has limited flow, you know that water is not getting to the filter adequately maybe because there is a suction leak in the lines or valves. It could simply be that the owner or some other person has adjusted the valves to limit flow on the suction side, or the lines that go to the suction side of the pump are restricted or clogged. This requires inspection of the skimmer baskets to see if they have something in them or that they are plugged with leaves and junk that would limit the flow of water.

On a skimmer that has a floating weir, make sure that the weir, the inside part, is not stuck. If they have debris stuck in them or for some other unexplained reason, you need to correct that and recheck the system. Some skimmer baskets actually float up when the pump is not on, and then they tip letting everything that they have collected fall down to the bottom of the skimmer. So what happens when the pump starts for the next cycle? It sucks all that debris through the lines and into the pump trap basket, further limiting flow.

If those items are okay and working properly, shut off the pump and check the o-ring on the pump lid. Make sure it fits right and has no cracks in it. It should be pliable, and you should actually be able to squeeze it and cause it to flatten out a little. If it is old and starting to rot or is hard, replace it. If it is okay, make sure you clean it and all surfaces that it contacts and then lube it with a non-petroleum lube designed for pool o-rings and seals. Before you re-install the lid to the pump, check the trap itself to see if any particles are stuck in the hole that goes to the impeller. Do not stick your fingers into that hole until you have disabled the pump. Either make sure you have it shut off at the timing device, or better yet, shut the breaker off that leads to the pump.

Now I have a small swivel mirror that I carry so that I can actually look into the hole at the impeller opening to see if there is any debris in it. If I cannot see or feel any debris, I assume that the impeller is free of debris. This does not mean that it is, but it will save some time if I notice or feel obstructions and can remedy the situation before proceeding.

To clean an impeller you can refer to Chapter 10 for the motor replacement section to see how to remove the motor. You do not have to remove the impeller to clean it. You can take a small pointed pair of needle-nose pliers and pull all the debris out that you can take from the opening at the center of the impeller. Then you can take a piece of wire, like 14 gauge electrical solid core wire, and push it in the reverse flow of water through the veins in the outer portion of the impeller. You want to try to push it back the way it came. Trying to push it through the impeller from the center to the outer part may only pack the debris tighter. The tighter that the debris is packed, the harder it is to get out.

Photos

All photos taken by author Dan Hardy of Rick Lorick Pools.
Photos courtesy of Rick Lorick.

Photo 1 - Large modern pool
An impressive party pool in Ocala's horse country.

Photo 2
Freeform pool

This pool has a rock waterfall and built-in slide.

Photo 3

Basic rectangular pool

Photo 4

Pool under construction

This pool is waiting for a deck and a surface.

Photo 5

Pool under construction

New pool with tile and deck ready for surface to be applied.

Photo 6

Pool ready for surfacing

This is a new pool ready for surface. Note the pipes in the floor are part of a floor cleaning system called a Caretaker.

Photo 7

Filled and finished pool

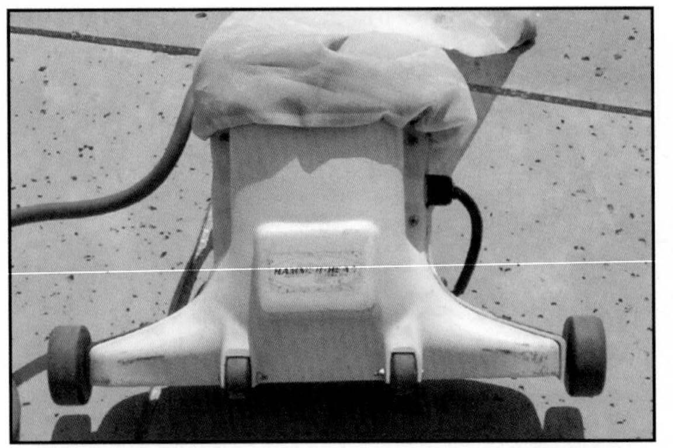

Photo 8

Hammerhead cleaner

A very used pool cleaner with its own power supply.

Photo 9

Phantom cleaner

A Hayward phantom cleaner skimming the surface of a pool of debris. This is a pressure cleaner that has its own booster pump.

Photo 10

Vanishing edge (1)

Pool with 40′ vanishing edge and spa.

Photo 11

Vanishing edge (2)

Water overflowing on the vanishing edge into a pit for recirculation.

Photo 12

Standard valve

This two-way valve is made by Intermatic. It can turn a line totally off or on. It can also adjust flow to a desired amount. This particular valve can have an actuator mounted on it to activate it automatically.

Photo 13

Spa with television

This portable spa has a flat screen television and a marine stereo system. This spa has four pumps and many features.

Photo 14

Pool and spa combination

Multi-colored one-inch tiles in shallow area for children make a pretty pattern.

Photo 15

Finished and filled pool

Photo 16

Pool with spa, fountain, and waterfall

Photo 17 - Finished and filled pool

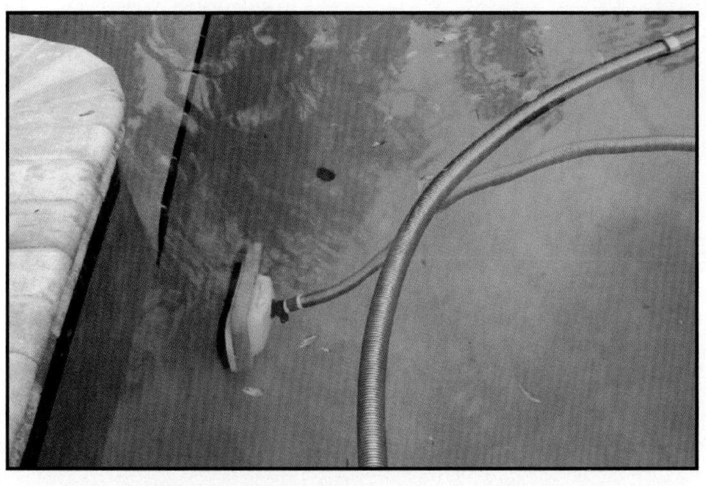

Photo 18 - Suction cleaner

This one is climbing the walls in moderate leaves.

Photo 19 - Screened pool
A screen solves many cleaning problems.

Photo 20 - Screened pool

At this point, our pump impeller is free from obstruction, and it still does not flow water well. Before now I probably would have replaced the gauge on the filter with a gauge that I know is working well. A new gauge does not mean it is a good gauge. If the gauge is wrong and the pressure is high, follow the instructions in Chapter 10 for cleaning the filter that you have. If it is reading the same pressure as the original one did, the problem may not be the filter.

If all the equipment seems to be functioning, the problem could be cavitations or sucking air. If you look at the lid of the pump, you can see whether there are bubbles in the water, and if there are bubbles, there is a good chance that you have a suction leak in either the pump, the lines, or the valves. In Chapter 10, I also explain how you can use electrical tape to find a suction leak in the fittings at the pump and at all connections on the suction side. If a suction leak is detected, you must repair it first, prime, and restart the pump.

If there is a rolling motion inside the trap or it has a roaring sound, it could be cavitations. Cavitations can be caused by too big a pump that is not allowing enough water to enter it. It is also a sign of a restriction to the pressure side or outflow side that is limiting the flow of water that creates the vacuum. Since the filter should be the first piece of equipment that is plumbed from the pump, any restriction after the filter should raise the pressure of the water on the pressure gauge. That would also apply to a return line if it was restricted or turned down.

You notice I said "should" in that last paragraph. Over the years I have run into a couple of strange things. A filter can actually be really plugged and read low pressure because it will not let the pump prime all the way causing cavitations by not allowing the flow of water to create enough vacuum in the pump.

In a centrifugal pump as the flow of water starts to increase, it pulls the water through the impeller causing more suction. Limiting this flow can cause the pump to have cavitations. If the flow of water is not sufficient, the pressure will not rise. If enough water can pass through the plugged filter media and not cause a restriction of flow, it will not register as high pressure. I have seen this happen only three times, and it really does not make any sense. These symptoms happened on grid DE filters, and the problem was cured by backwashing the filter.

Another weird one is that the system has a lack of backpressure (restrictions) causing the water to be forced out faster than it can suck water in because of improper size of pipe or pump. If a pump is restricted by the pipe's being too small for the amount of water the pump needs to take in, the water can leave the pump easier than it can be pulled in. After running a while, sometimes the flow can come to an equal point and work properly. When this occurs, a two-way valve needs to be installed in the return line and slightly closed to get enough backpressure to overcome this problem. It is very similar to having a restriction in the lines but is harder to find.

Now that we have walked around the equipment and checked for proper operation, if the pool is equipped with a chlorine generator, you want to look at the control panel for any error messages and the salt level of the pool. If the salt level is low or high, it will alert you to a problem that you may notice during the testing for a chlorine residue in the water.

At this point, take a good look at the pool. You should look for staining on the walls or discoloration of the water. You will be able to tell if the water is cloudy or clear. If it is a pool that you regularly take care of, you should be able to see some change in the look of the water and pool.

Some of the things that you look for are air bubbles coming out of the returns, telling you that air is getting into the system from somewhere. You can view how the pool is actually flowing and see whether it has enough flow. Your inspection will cover looking at the main drain to see whether it is properly secured and if all the return nozzles are there. If the pool has an automatic cleaner, you can watch the operation of the cleaner. You can observe quite a bit just by looking at a pool. What you are doing is making a plan of attack on how to take care of this pool.

It is time to clean the pool. The first thing that I do is to take a water sample. It is best to take a sample after the pool has run for a while so that everything is in good circulation and solution. You take a sample from about 18 inches deep and away from a return keeping you from getting an inaccurate reading on the sanitizer level if the pool is equipped with a chlorinator of some type. Taking a sample from the return will show you whether chlorine is being introduced into the pool but will not show the accurate level that is in solution.

Next, I like to clean the tiles. There are many tile cleaners on the market. Some are acid based and some are not. The acid based products will clean scale and stains off the tile and grout better, but you have to be careful and not let them set too long since the acid will eat away the grout. Also, if the brush drips this acid solution on the deck, it can damage the paint or stain the surface. The bucket is a good parking place for your tile brush after you use it so you do not damage anything.

Make sure to select a tile soap that fits your exact need. For instance, you do not use a tile soap designed for a concrete pool to clean a vinyl or fiberglass pool. You can damage the surfaces of the fiberglass or ruin the liner.

The soap should do a couple of things. It should clean the debris and oils that have attached themselves to the surface at the water line so that it is clean and the debris does not damage the surface. It also will make it harder for small debris to reattach itself to the surface, and you can skim the removed debris off easily with your leaf rake or skimmer net.

Next, I skim the surface of the pool to allow me to vacuum the pool without any of the floating debris sinking into an area that I have already vacuumed. The debris floating on top of the water will show up as shadows on the bottom of the pool. Sometimes it is hard to determine whether something is on the bottom. What you have to do when vacuuming a pool is to fill the hose with water so that the pump does not suck air. This is simple. Hook the vacuum head onto the pool pole. Attach the swivel end of your pool hose to the vacuum head, if it has one, and lower the vacuum head into the pool. Position it so that the vacuum does not roll causing you to lose the head and pool pole in the water. With this in place, simply force the hose down straight into the water to let water fill the hose and remove all the air from the hose. When the hose is full, keep it at the water line and install it into the cleaner port, skimmer hole, or if you are using a skim plate or vacuum plate, it goes on top of the skimmer basket.

You would use the cleaner port or skimmer hole to vacuum only if the pool has sediment on the bottom and very little debris. This debris will go straight to the pump trap basket, which is the last stop for larger debris before entering the pump. I strongly recommend that you use a vacuum plate. Even if the pool is clean looking, things can be in the pool that can damage the trap basket. It can be even more devastating if the line is clogged with something that you did not see.

Small rocks or marbles can actually gain enough speed and force going through the lines that they can crack or break the basket in the trap of the pump. If a ping-pong ball gets into the lines, you will have real problems. Balloon pieces and plastic are bad for trapping other smaller debris that would normally go through without any problem. Therefore, for your benefit it is strongly recommended that you use a skim plate or vacuum plate.

After you get the pool hose hooked up with the pump running, you can start vacuuming. To get enough suction pressure you may have to adjust your suction valves. It is a good thing to turn off your drain valves. If you have multiple skimmers, you may have to adjust them also to get a good head of suction. One of the reasons is that when you add another 35′ of suction hose to the system, it is another 35′ that the pump has to pull water through. You can tell when you have enough suction by the resistance that it puts on the vacuum by sucking it down hard to the floor of the pool and by watching the debris on the floor of the pool. If you move the vacuum over debris and you see it scatter, you either have too little suction or you are moving the vacuum head too fast. Experience will teach you the speed of vacuuming and the proper suction pressure needed. It is on-the-job training. You need to vacuum the entire bottom of the pool and come up the wall with the vacuum to remove debris that is loosely attached to the pool walls.

You may ask why I do not sweep the walls first before vacuuming. If you sweep the walls, the particles are not going to drop immediately to the floor of the pool. They are going to try to go into solution and will be floating around the pool while you are vacuuming. If you vacuum the walls also, you remove the loose debris and limit the amount of floating debris for the filter to take out. After vacuuming the pool, you sweep the walls from the top to the bottom. Now you have a pool that is clean.

On pools with algae, the procedure is different. Cleaning around the returns and in corners and all fixtures is important to keep algae from forming and sediments from staining that area. Dead spots are the worst areas where algae and staining can occur most frequently.

After the vacuuming is done, I recheck the filter pressure to see if cleaning is needed. I skim the surface of the pool again, test the sample of water that I had taken earlier, and adjust the chemical levels. A good idea is to clean off the deck of the pool so that the debris does not blow into the pool you just cleaned. You can sweep it, wash it off with water, or use a blower. I do not like blowers since they stir up small particles and phosphates, and they float around in the air and deposit themselves into the water. A pool is a magnet for anything that is in the air.

After this is all done and you have cleaned up the area, put the tools back into your vehicle, and completed your paperwork, there is one last step. You need to leave a note for the customers to let them know what their levels were and notify them of the chemicals that you have put into the pool. Let them know when it is safe to go back into the pool. If you shock a pool, it is important for the customers to know that they cannot get into the water until the level is safe. This is the time to take a last look at the equipment to see if you put it back to the proper adjustments that are needed to have the pool function at its maximum efficiency. Many problems can be solved by doing a final walkthrough, and you will be surprised at what you may find. This quick procedure can eliminate complaints about something that may look different or that is not performing the way it should. An example is the automatic cleaner being adjusted properly and working the way it was designed. Water features that are not functioning as they were means the client will call you right away.

When the tiles have deposits on them, it takes a little more work. You have to be careful with the tile so that you do not damage them. Before applying any product, read the instructions first. Some products can damage tile and grout. Marble is actually soft and can be damaged by some products. When using a new product, always test a small area in a hidden spot to see what reaction you get.

If the choice has been made to scrape the scale or deposits off the tile using a scraper or putty knife, use caution. Cheaper quality tiles can be damaged by scraping. Using a wire brush can also damage tiles. This is the time to use patience and be careful. One of the main problems with damaging tile on the pool is not replacing it: it is matching it. Going to your local tile shop for tile that was installed 10 years earlier will always result in dissatisfaction. Designs come and go and are hard to find after a short time.

If the tiles have algae on the area between the tile and the surface or on the top of the tile between the tile and deck, it requires a different approach. Usually black algae grow in those areas. You need to scrub the algae-infested areas lightly with a stainless steel brush to break the protective barrier of the algae. Then you need to apply a strong concentration of chlorine to kill the algae. I dip a soft bristle brush into a concentrated chlorine product, usually trichlor, and apply it to the algae. It works fast to kill the algae. Once you have encountered algae in this area, you need to keep an eye on it to see if it returns.

My experience has been that if algae has formed on the top of the tiles, it could be anywhere. Tile on a pool is usually installed differently than the tile on the floor of your home. Instead of a solid coat of adhesive, only a small spot is used on the tile to hold it in place, leaving voids. In these voids algae can thrive. I have actually raised the water level to the top of the tiles and used silver algaecide to treat the pool. After 72 hours of constant running of the circulation pump, I drain the pool down to normal and see what happens. If all goes well the silver algaecide will kill the algae and no repeat of infestation will occur. This is one of those areas where experience is the key to success.

The key to trying things is to use your head and realize the effect your action has on other things. You may think that my claim of not wanting to use many chemicals is incorrect. I do hate to put poisons in water where people gather to have fun. Sometimes it is necessary to use the most powerful chemical to achieve a goal. Knowing when to give up the traditional treatments and go for the gold is a decision one has to make. I cannot tell you what to use and when to use it without looking at the problem. I can only share some of my experiences with you to help you decide how to proceed.

The moral to this story is to document what you do with a particular problem. Things repeat themselves. Each pool will tell you what it needs if you let it. The trick to this business is to control the pool and not let it control you. I enjoy new challenges to break up the everyday routine. Weekly inspection of a pool will alert you to oncoming problems. You simply have to look at it.

CHAPTER 5

Chemicals and Cures

OVERVIEW

This section will go into the basic chemicals that are used to balance water and some tricks that I have learned over the years of taking care of pools and spas. I will cover spas in a later chapter since I feel they require a better understanding and care because of being a small body of water.

The guidelines that are set by different agencies are designed for the safety of people who swim and use a spa. Sometimes we tweak the levels, but only by understanding what the consequences are. Too many people take the art of balancing a pool as "not rocket science." However, when the health and well being of the human body is at stake, we take it very seriously, and for those "experts" who know it all, particular attention should be given to adding chemicals to water. Never add something that you just want to try because you ran out of options. Problems that can occur with the misuse of pool chemicals can turn deadly, and we take them very seriously.

Almost every chemical you add to your pool or spa can have an effect on some other aspect of the balance of water. If all water were almost perfect, balancing would be no problem. I was told once that there were more than 250 things that were in water that could affect the chemistry. I do not know for sure exactly how accurate that is, but each pool is different. Whenever you add a chemical to adjust one thing, you can be sure that it has an effect on another thing. Balancing is an art and a science. Nothing feels better than to take an ugly mess of sludge and algae and transform it into brilliant clear water. Recently on a Wednesday, I was asked to clean a pool so that they could have a pool party for the son of the owners' birthday on Friday. That is pushing even a halfway decent pool. As I approached the pool, I noticed it had a bad case of mustard algae, and it was half drained. The pool pole was in the pool and attached was the vacuum head and the hose. All you could see was the top part of the hose cuff and the rest was submerged in about three inches of yellow muck. At that point, the decision was easy. With most of the water gone, the best solution was to drain the pool.

There are several considerations to deal with in this situation. Pumping the type of algae in this state onto someone's yard or in the street poses problems. Pumping it into the street could surely cause stains from the algae on the roadway and gutter and would most likely contaminate any water that it merged with. We have a lot of storm drainage ponds all over, and contaminating them was not an option.

There is no alternative but to get radical. The estimated amount of water in the pool was 8,000 gallons. I added one pound of sodium bromide and since it takes some kind of catalyst to activate this I hit it hard with four pounds of calcium hypochloride. Since I have explained that the lower the pH, the better chlorine works, I added only half a gallon of muriatic acid to the mix before I put in the other chemicals.

Mixing large amounts of chemicals in a small volume of water without waiting for a certain time is not the safest thing to do. I was on a short schedule. I had left my submersible pump at home and it took about an hour to go and get it and return. Before I left, I took my pool pole with my brush and stirred the water around to mix this toxic mess I had created. Upon my return, I got the result I had hoped for: fairly clear water. Another decision had to be made. Do I pump this highly acidic water with a mixture of chlorine and bromide onto this beautiful lawn. As you will learn later in the chapter, bromine or bromide will eat up chlorine. We added some sodium thiosulfate to help neutralize the chlorine, and then threw in two pounds of soda ash to help with the acidic problem. We stirred the pot with the brush and then fired up the submersible pump. Once the level got down to about six inches, I went in and removed the main drain cover and set the pump in the drain to get every last drop of water out of the pool that I could.

I had to make a decision on the next procedure. I had algae on the pool walls and on the floor. I mixed a bucket of about three gallons of water to two pounds of calcium hypochlorite until it dissolved. I took that and scrubbed the walls and floor of the pool, rinsed it down with fresh water, added a little more sodium thiosulfate, and pumped this water out of the pool. The next step is not the smartest, but I have learned to run while holding my breath. Here I have a drained pool with some areas that really need to be acid washed. Usually the best attack after a good rinsing is to let the pool air dry for a day in full sun to evaporate the chlorine. I chose to take a chance and try to make this pool a little more presentable for the birthday boy. I will get into the acid washing section later. I started doing a small section to see what kind of reaction I would get between the leftover chlorine residue and the acid mixed at about three parts water to one part acid. Most of the sections I chose to do were going really well until I got down to the deep end on the floor where more chlorine had been used and still had chlorine residue that didn't get pumped out. When I smelled that smell and saw that smoke, I was out of there. That reaction is chlorine gas, and it will kill you—not real wise, but I did know what to look for and was taking it slow since I was expecting some type of reaction. What I can tell you from this experience, which really was not a close call, is to do as I tell you and not as I do. People die from pushing their luck. I had a nice, even breeze, and it was a cool day. If it had been a hot day or the pool color was dark, virtually turning it into an oven, my decision would have been to wait. Don't push your luck dealing with chemicals. They will usually win, and that may be why there are not great numbers of older pool professionals around.

WHAT WATER WANTS, IT USUALLY GETS

The best way for me to explain this is if the water needs something, it will attempt to take it from whatever is available. If it needs a little calcium, it might attempt to take it from the surface of the pool by pitting or etching the surface. If it needs to get rid of something like scale, it has no problem depositing it wherever it can. It is called balance. You have to balance the water to give the water what it needs to keep it from doing damage and to protect the pool and its equipment. Therefore, either you keep the water in good balance, or the water will take over and do whatever it wants to. It is called **BALANCE AND DEMAND.**

SANITIZERS

A sanitizer is a chemical or device that kills or inactivates microorganisms present in pool and spa water. There are a few different types of chlorine and bromine, the most popular choices. Other sanitizers include ozone, biguanide (PHMB), copper and/or silver ionization, and UV radiation. That definition is from Taylor Technologies, and it describes it well.

Chlorine acts as a sanitizer, destroys microorganisms, and acts as an oxidizer. Oxidation is described as the burning up of organic contaminants that have been introduced into the water, such as deodorant, suntan lotions, body oils, perspiration, pollen, dirt, and leaves.

Now microorganisms and organics consume chlorine. This is called chlorine demand and has a basic definition of the amount of chlorine that will be needed to react with these contaminants before any chlorine is left unreacted.

The causes of this demand are that microorganisms are living creatures that can only be seen through a microscope. They are introduced by rain, wind, humans, and dogs. They consist of algae, bacteria, fungi, protozoans, yeast, and viruses. Yes, even viruses have been found in water that is unsanitized. Most of these organisms in pool water are harmless to us, but others cause disease and infection. These germs can be transmitted from one person to another through water. The reason for balancing and sanitizing water is not just to make it a pretty blue.

A study at Harvard University concluded that one active adult swimmer loses two pints of perspiration per hour. Perspiration is loaded with compounds resembling urine. With the combination of these things and nasal discharge, fecal matter, and urine, you begin to appreciate the need to sanitize.

I have talked with hundreds of parents, and I try to explain this in the best way I can. Not one person will admit that their child urinates in the swimming pool. Now I cannot speak for the opposite sex, but when a little boy jumps into the pool and comes in contact with cool water, his bladder empties. This is ammonia. It makes chloramines.

The definition of chloramines is any combination of nitrogen or ammonia and chlorine. They control the release of chlorine and are slow to do so. Therefore super chlorination or what we call shocking is performed. This will be described in detail later.

In sanitation, chlorine comes in two forms: stabilized and unstabilized. Of the six chlorinating chemicals, four are classified as unstabilized. They are described below.

CHLORINE GAS

We call the people who use chlorine gas "bottle jockeys" because gas comes out of compressed bottles of chlorine. Not that many suppliers of bottles are left around, at least in Florida, because of safety concerns. Advantages are that it is reported to be the least expensive form of chlorine. It is the purest form with an available chlorine content of 100 percent. It is extremely dangerous to handle and it lowers the pH level dramatically, destroys total alkalinity levels, and has a high base demand. It is used on larger commercial pools.

Chlorine gas is heavier than air. It will sit on the top of water. A couple of years ago in South Florida, a bottle jockey administered chlorine gas into a pool. The method is to stick a wand into the pool, release the gas, and remove the wand from the water. If the wand has not purged itself of all the gas, when it is pulled out of the water, the excess gas will sit on the surface.

A couple of young boys dived into the pool after the pool man drove away and as they came out of the water to get that much needed breath, they inhaled the chlorine gas, which killed them.

Chlorine gas was the first chemical used in the gas chamber to execute criminals beginning in 1924. In April of 1915, the German Army used it against the British and Canadians in Belgium. The gas destroyed the respiratory organs of its victims leading to a slow death by asphyxiation, a horrible way to die. It was found that if soldiers covered their mouths with a cloth soaked in urine (ammonia), it neutralized the chlorine gas. This tells you how the effect of ammonia in the water can kill the chlorine in your pool.

Chlorine gas has an active strength of 100 percent with a pH of 0 in a 1 percent solution.

CALCIUM HYPOCHLORITE

Non-stabilized chlorine is commonly known as Cal Hypo, HTH, and by other names. It is solid granular chlorine that has a moderate solubility. It also is being manufactured in tablet form. Made in various strengths from 45 percent to 78 percent active strength, it usually has a pH factor of 8.5 to 11.8 that varies from manufacturer to manufacturer.

Because of its low price it is the most used shocking agent. It is slow to dissolve, but the negative part is that it does leave considerable sediments after the chlorine enters the water. The use of Cal Hypo raises your TDS.

Cal Hypo is better distributed by mixing in water before pouring into a pool. Pre-dissolving prevents some staining that can appear on certain surfaces. However, it will eat holes in your clothes if there is any contact.

Cal Hypo will support combustion and one needs to avoid mixing it with acids, ammonia, soda pop, oil, trichlor, or just about anything but water. Mixing with organics will cause a fire. Putting Cal Hypo tablets or granular in the chlorinator used for Trichlor will cause a chemical explosion, usually resulting in fire with injuries or possibly death. Never mix chemicals.

SODIUM HYPOCHLORITE

Commonly known as LIQUID CHLORINE, it is very cost effective. Negative factors are that if you spill it on your clothes or in your car, they are history.

Sodium hypochlorite is a chemical compound with the formula NaOCI. A solution of sodium hypochlorite is frequently called "bleach," and is used as a disinfectant and bleaching agent.

Sodium hypochlorite is a strong oxidizer, and the products of the oxidation reactions are corrosive. They can burn the skin and cause eye damage, particularly when used in concentrated forms. Hypochlorite must not be mixed with organic materials (such as dirt) since the resulting trihalomethanes (also called haloforms) are carcinogenic. The extent of the hazard thus created is a subject of disagreement.

Hypochlorite should never be mixed with another household

cleaner, especially not with those containing acid, since the mix generates chlorine gas. It should also never be mixed with anything containing ammonia, since the combination results in chloramine gas. Chloramine gas and chlorine gas are highly toxic. It also reacts with hydrogen peroxide.

Now this poor chemical has been through the government wringer for sure. It is a disinfectant, a pesticide, listed as corrosive, and who knows what else it will be listed under because it has so many uses. Experts don't have a clue how to classify it.

Besides the low concentration of available chlorine, sodium hypochlorite also greatly increases the TDS and has an extremely high pH of 13.

I like liquid chlorine because it is so easy to use. Just pour it in and it does the rest. It goes into solution almost instantly and leaves no visible residue. Great product!

LITHIUM HYPOCHLORITE

Lithium is the safest of all the chlorines to handle, but is also the most expensive. There is not much use of this chemical because of the price. It has a large inert content, making it high in TDS.

Lithium is one of the more recently developed forms of chlorine. It is produced by bubbling chlorine gas through a solution of lithium, sodium, and potassium sulfates. When dried, the result is a free-flowing powder that provides only 35 percent available chlorine.

Lithium is calcium free, dust free, and non-flammable. It has a long shelf life, and because it contains no calcium, it dissolves rapidly without clouding or raising calcium levels. Because it dissolves so rapidly, it cannot be used in a dry-chlorine feeder and must be applied by hand. It has a high pH of 10.7, and neutralizing it requires about four ounces of muriatic acid per pound of lithium hypochlorite—different from the other chlorines and is a good shock for vinyl pools since it is so fast-dissolving.

CYANURATES - TRICHLOR AND DICHLOR

Cyanurates basically means that cyanuric acid is part of the mixture and that the chlorine is stabilized. The two cyanurates are trichloro-trianzinetrione, called trichlor, and sodium dichloro-s-triazinetrione, called dichlor.

TRICHLOR

Trichlor comes in granular and tablet form. We consider sticks as being tablet form.

Trichlor is designed for the cooler water of swimming pools and contains a high percentage (90 percent) of available chlorine. Trichlor should never be used in a spa as the high temperatures will cause it to dissolve very quickly. It comes in a one-inch tablet, three-inch tablet, a stick, cartridge, or granular. It does have a long shelf life, and it is very slow to dissolve in cool water, allowing it to work extremely well in swimming pool floaters and erosion-type feeders.

Trichlor has a very low pH of 2.9 and requires frequent monitoring and adjustment of pH to prevent damage to equipment and other metal parts.

Trichlor is produced through drying and cooling sodium salt of cyanuric acid in the presence of chlorine gas. The resulting compound provides 90 percent available chlorine.

DICHLOR

Sodium Dichlor is the only type of chlorine that should be used in a spa. It is fast dissolving, will not cloud the water, is relatively pH neutral, and has a long shelf life. Because of its granular makeup, there is no way to dispense it automatically; therefore, it must be added by hand.

Sodium dichlor is chemically produced by adding soda ash and cyanuric acid to a solution of trichlor. When dried, the result is a granule that provides from 56 percent to 97 percent available chlorine, depending on the method of manufacture.

The drawback is that dichlor is expensive.

CHLORAMINES

When chlorine is added to water, it generally forms hypochlorous acid, the powerful killing form of chlorine, and a hypochlorite ion, a relatively weak form of chlorine. The percentage of hypochlorous acid and hypochlorite ions is determined by the pH of the water. As the pH goes up, less of the chlorine is in the killing form and more of the chlorine is in the weaker form. The total of hypochlorous acid and hypochlorite ions is the free available chlorine. A general rule is that a pH of around 7.2 lets the chlorine work at 80 percent and a pH of 7.8 restricts the chlorine effectiveness to 20 percent.

Chlorine can combine with ammonia and nitrogen compounds in the water to form chloramines, also called "combined chlorine." By combining with ammonia and nitrogen, free chlorine in the water is disabled. Chloramines are 60 to 80 times less effective than free chlorine and are formed any time ammonia and nitrogen are in the water. Some of the ammonia and nitrogen compounds are introduced into the water by bathers in the form of perspiration, urine, and saliva. Ammonia and nitrogen compounds are also introduced into the water by rain. Each drop of rain has some dissolved nitrogen from the atmosphere. That is why your lawn looks so good after a good rain.

Chloramines not only smell bad; they are eye and skin irritants, and they can cloud the water. Another tip from on old timer: if you smell chlorine in the pool, usually you do not have enough free chlorine and it is locked up making chloramines and super chlorination. Super chlorination or shocking needs to be performed.

SUPER CHLORINATION (SHOCKING)

Commonly called breakpoint chlorination or shocking. It is basically the addition of high amounts of chlorine to destroy chloramines and unwanted bacteria and algae.

Removing chloramines takes a dose of chlorine that raises the levels to 10 times the level of combined chlorines for a minimum of four hours. A ratio of 7.6 to 1 must be achieved of chlorine to chloramines.

A nonchlorine product called potassium monopersulfate can be used to destroy choramines, but IT WILL NOT kill algae.

Potassium monosulfate is also a good shock for spas that are using bromine.

In a spa, an ozone generator will reduce and maybe eliminate the need to shock. Each time the ammonia and nitrogen enter the ozonated water, they are oxidized by the ozone.

My rule of thumb is this. I always shock a pool whether it is to get rid of chloramines or algae. For a basic shock, you want 30 to 50 parts per million of chlorine. That will destroy good hard algae. If algae are not visible, I limit it to around 30 ppm. If a good algae bloom is present, I hammer it with 50 ppm.

Some say that when you shock a pool using liquid chlorine and add anhydrous ammonia with the liquid chlorine, it forms nitrogen. Nitrogen—commonly called nitrates—and phosphates are nutrients for algae. When the algae eat the nitrogen, they also take in the chloramines, and it kills them. I know that it works, but purchasing anhydrous ammonia means you are carrying another hazardous chemical. Anhydrous ammonia forms an alkali when in contact with water, and it chemically burns skin tissue. The chemical will burn its way into the body unless it is diluted by vast quantities of water. Skin cells are reduced to a sticky, gooey substance as the chemical burn progresses. The skin cells are actually killed and are not capable of healing or replacing themselves. Damaged tissue must be removed by a medical doctor so that healing can proceed. The results can often be disfiguring. You can see why I am not interested in carrying anhydrous ammonia. Just call me "Chicken."

Charts are provided to help you figure out the dosage of superchlorination.

Good news for the professional and the pool owner: many of the salt generators that produce chlorine have the capability to shock the pool to get rid of chlorimines. They are not designed to kill a bloom of algae. More discussion on that later.

CHLORINE ALTERNATIVES OR OTHER CHEMICALS

There are several different alternatives to chlorine, but I will go into only a few, since the others are rarely used. They are not economical and most do not do what their labels say they will do.

In my professional opinion, when you see an advertisement for a product that says chlorine free, be cautious. Most reduce the amount of chlorine that has to be used, but when you figure the cost, you wind up paying more for the product or the system.

BROMINE

The chemical name for the brominating tablets that we use in pools and spas is bromochloro-5, 5 dimethylhydantoin. You can see why they just call it bromine.

Bromine is a reddish brown liquid. If you look at the chemical name on the brominating tablets, you will notice chloro right behind the bromo. That is because bromine needs chlorine or some other catalyst to activate it. Therefore, they just add a little chlorine to the mix and you have a chemical that will activate when put in water. Normal bromine tablets have 61 percent bromine and 27 percent chlorine. This also differs by different manufacturers.

People who think they are chlorine-free are wrong. You could achieve that with different bromine products and adding a nonchlorine alternative like potassium monopersulfate, will activate the bromine. Bromine costs more than chlorine, and by doing the two-step method, costs would get out of hand.

Like chlorine, bromine produces amines. These are called bromamines which turn out to be far more carcinogenic (cancer causing) than chloramines. Even trace amounts of bromine can trigger severe acne in sensitive individuals. Even though it is a good algaecide, there are some forms of organisms, most notably forms of either a black fungi or algae, according to some anecdotal reports, that are not susceptible to bromine. In other words, some algae are resistant to bromine products, and it will not kill them.

Although both chlorine and bromine are halogens, which means salt-forming, bromine is more stable and less volatile in water than chlorine. Less of the bromine escapes the water as a gas because it has a very high evaporation point. That is what makes it so desirable in a heated spa.

Since bromine tablets already have their own oxidizer, chlorine, it is not necessary to use a separate catalyst. This combination makes hypobromous acid and when joined with a contaminant it becomes a bromine ion. The buildup of these ions in the water forms what is called a bromine bank. There is an old saying, "once a bromine pool, always a bromine pool." If a level of bromine ions present in the water is 15 ppm or more, all the chlorine added is going toward converting bromide ions into hypobromous acid and none of it will provide chlorine residual. That is the reason when you use sodium bromide as an algaecide, it eats up so much chlorine. Once the level of bromine drops below 15 ppm, chlorine can start to produce its own hypochlorous acid.

Just remember that any addition of bromine to a chlorine sanitized pool or spa can render it unstable. We will dig a little deeper in the spa chapter.

POTASSIUM MONOPERSULFATE (PM)

PM is a free flowing, white granular solid, soluble in water. It is present as a component of a triple salt including potassium monopersulfate, potassium sulfate, and potassium bisulfate.

The compound provides a powerful nonchlorine oxidation for many uses. I use it for a shock in bromine pool and spas. We occasionally use an algaecide for mustard and black algae, sodium bromide, which we will get deeply into later. It is a good algaecide for mustard and initial forms of black algae, but it needs a catalyst to activate it. Chorine can be used, but for those people who do not like chlorine, potassium monopersulfate is a good alternative.

It is used very much for shocking vinyl pools for the removal of chloramines. It will not kill algae by itself. For pools, shocking weekly with one to two pounds per 10,000 gallons of water will take care of most chloramines. It does vary with the bather load of the pool.

Now for spas, it should be added to spa water after every use at a dose of about one to two ounces per 250 gallons, to immediately oxidize and eliminate organic contaminates introduced by bathers. If the spa has an ozonator, shocking is not needed after every use, provided that the system runs for a while afterwards so that the ozone is circulated through the system.

BIGUANICIDES

Common names are Baquacil. This is a product that I do not like—not to say it is a bad product, but it is expensive to use and in Florida, if you do not add new water every year, you develop problems.

I helped a competitor change his display pools from Baquacil to chlorine because of problems they had on their show lot. The Baquacil people could not eliminate the problems and blamed it on being too close to a major highway. Here is my opinion. I have had people tell me that in the Northern states it works very well in pools and spas. I will let you be the judge of it if you ever encounter a pool or spa with this product.

It is not compatible with chlorine or bromine. Put chlorine in a pool being treated with biguanicides, and it will turn to what looks like brownish gravy. If you take on a pool sanitized by this product, do not use the same cleaning tools that you use on chlorine or bromine pools. Cross-contamination will occur and you will have a mess on your hands.

ALGAECIDES AND ALGAESTATS

Now an algaecide is used to kill algae and an algaestat is used to prevent algae. Many algaecides should be called algaestats because they have poor killing abilities. They are just too weak.

When an algaecide is used in a pool, less chlorine can be used for water purification, resulting in water that is more pleasant to swim in without the stinging eyes and nose. Regular use of algaecides also prolongs the life of water filtration systems as there is less plant material to clog the filters and intakes of the pump.

This advice you can follow or not: I do not like a lot of chemicals in pools. A good sanitizing routine can control most problems, but you still can get algae with good balanced water. This is where your knowledge of the particular pool you own or are taking care of comes in. If a pool is prone to a problem for many reasons, a preventive measure is good. Make sure that all equipment is working properly because as previously stated, filtration is the key to preventing many problems, including some algae.

Just about every manufacturer who makes any type of chemical for swimming pools or spas has their own brand of algaecide. It is important that you look at the label of each product to determine the strength and in the case of metal algaecides, find out whether manufacturers have their own chelating agent as part of their formula. You will notice that discount products are usually very weak.

If the product works following the recommended dosage, more will not help; they will simply cause more problems. This is especially true with metal algaecides. More does not mean better.

I never found quaternary ammonium compounds effective at all, and they are not readily available in this area of Florida because no one wants to buy them except at discount stores.

They are common algaecides in a liquid form and contain from 1 percent to more than 20 percent effective ingredients. These algaecides are not to be used in place of regular disinfectants, as they are ineffective against many bacteria, and they cause foaming. They can react dangerously with soaps and detergents. If you have ever used one of these and witnessed the foaming that you get from these products, you will not use them again. They are popular with discount stores.

POLYMERS

Polymers are substances whose molecules have high molar masses and are composed of large number of repeating units. There are both natural and synthetic polymers. Among naturally occurring polymers are proteins, starches, cellulose, and latex.

They are formed by chemical reactions that create a chain of molecules called monomers and are joined sequentially. They can use only one monomer or a variety. Confused? It means that polymers basically replicate each other repeatedly.

Polymers attempt to surround algae and smother it. Actually, they try to surround anything in the pool and smother it. The more debris you have in the pool, the less effective the poly algaecide is because it tries to trap everything that floats.

Good manufacturers will advertise this type of algaecide primarily for green algae. Chlorine kills green algae. So why use polymers?

Polymers are ineffective against some mustard algae and black algae. The reason is that yellow or mustard algae usually has a protective slime covering and black algae has a protective shell that usually requires brushing with a stainless steel brush to break the "crust," as I call it and let the product work. They are not good for preventive measures either, but they are available because of negative propaganda about metal algaecides.

These algaecides are available in retail franchise stores rather than in the warehouses that professionals use. They also come in different strengths such as 30, 50, and 60. You will pay almost as much for a 30 percent poly as you will for a 60 percent poly. They may have some purpose and may work for what they were designed for, but in my business time is money, and algae that is allowed to take over the surface of the pool can do damage that I will not allow.

COPPER ALGAECIDE

Copper algaecide is most effective in a 7 percent solution. It will kill all kinds of algae and is recommended in darker pools but not recommended in pools with a salt generator because of the possibility of plating the generating cell. The active ingredient is copper sulfate.

Copper algaecide basically smothers the algae. It is very poisonous and will stain if you spill it on the deck. A good quality of copper algaecide will not stain the pool walls and will prevent algae from forming if a maintenance dose is used. Like all metals, as time goes on, some staining has to occur.

Sun Pool Products makes a very good copper algaecide that contains a chelating agent that helps prevent staining by keeping the metal in solution. If you use copper algaecide in a light colored pool to kill the algae blooms that are tucked away in the light niche or in the line somewhere, a metal-removing chemical might be added to remove the copper from the water as a preventive from staining, but your preventive measures will be lost. It works well in vinyl and fiberglass pools where the staining factor is limited.

You have to mix or dilute copper in water to prevent the heavy metal from sinking to the bottom where it will stain. Dilute about eight ounces in three gallons of water or more and disperse it around the pool, being careful not to get it on anything. I like copper and have very good luck with it. Even though it costs a little more than other algaecides, it works. In the long run, it is cheaper to use once than to try several times to kill your algae bloom with other products.

Overdosing a pool with copper algaecide will turn the water the prettiest turquoise color you have ever seen. Now even though it looks good, I guarantee you the pool is staining. Getting copper to release from the pool once it has attached itself is very difficult. You will not have a happy owner. If you are called out to fix this problem, charge them well for not reading the label. (It should be a mandatory class in school to read the instructions and directions of everything you are working on.)

SILVER ALGAECIDE

I call this the big gun. It will kill all forms of algae in every condition and situation. Silver works like copper but does not carry the same side effects. However, it is harder to get because of governmental regulations. It is said that silver algaecide is sensitive to light and has damaged some pools. I have not seen that, but I usually apply it in the late afternoon when I have a chlorine level of about three ppm and just let the pool run. You will be surprised the next day what has happened.

Now just as with all chemicals, read the instructions and apply the proper amount. The way most silver algaecides are used is that you add eight ounces of silver in the skimmer. That is eight ounces and no more. When it comes out, it will be black. It scares some pool owners, but I knew a builder who used it in most of his new pools just to see how the water circulated, and then I applied that idea to pools. You can watch the circulation of the water when you use this product. Then you wait for 10 minutes before you add more. That is so the silver can get in solution so staining will not occur. DO NOT spill it on the deck. It will stain and you may not be able to wash it off.

After you have administered the proper amount according to the volume of the pool, leave the pump on and go home. When you return, you will be amazed at what this product has done. It is also a good product for salt generators, but it is not to be used as a preventive measure since we would prefer that our pool water contain no metals.

If you have a pool that continues to have serious yellow or black algae, this is the product to use. Also, most products will tell you that you can swim after an hour of putting this in the pool.

STAINS

Stains are some of the hardest problems for me to treat and cure. There are different chemicals for each type of stain. Most chemical manufacturers make a metal-removing chemical. Some are better than others, and most present other problems. Some companies make test kits to determine which type of stain you have, and they tell you which chemical to use on that particular stain.

Jack's Magic is a good product for stains. The manufacturer

has a test kit for testing and determining the type of stain and whether it can be removed. Like most products, they contain phosphates.

Most stains can be removed with acid also. The stains you get from leaves and nuts that fall off trees are usually tannic acid, found in hard woods. It can be removed by using citric acid. Tannic acid will also disappear after normal chlorination in several days. At that point, the surface should be swept very well.

Stain Master is a tool designed to siphon chemicals down a tube to a round head that fits into your pool pole. You can siphon muriatic acid down this hose and put concentrated acid on a spot, and it will dissolve. I have also used a piece of pipe and poured acid in the pipe and let it settle on the stain. If one attempt does not do anything, then discontinue. The acid can pit the surface even underwater.

SYNOPSIS

When choosing an algaecide, always read the label. Some algaecides that are advertised for black algae are nothing more than trichlor. If you have a few spots of black algae, which usually start as little dots in the pool, and can start anywhere, not just the shady side, you can add trichlor directly to the area after brushing, and it will be less expensive than buying their product. I know some people who actually put a chorine tablet on a black algae spot to kill it. It does work.

The moral of this story is that algae can damage surfaces and if you are in the business of taking care of pools, your time is very precious. If you play with ineffective products, it costs you and the pool owner time and money. You cannot make any money if you have to come back to a pool every day and babysit it for an algae problem. Use the right product, let the filter do its job, and continue working. Algae are not to be feared. It can occur even with the best balance of water, but it is the fun part of the business. You are competing against Mother Nature and nothing is more powerful than she is so that defeating her is a good feeling. I demand full control of my pools and I take better care of my customers' pools than I take care of my own.

For the professional, being referred by word of mouth from a customer to another person is the highest compliment that you can get. You are trusted to do a good job at a good price with no expense that is not needed. Remember that these products are all poison and your clients' safety is in your hands. Never let down the trust and safety of this profession.

Once you get a little experience under your belt, you will be able to recognize the chemical makeup of different products. Some products offered are simply the same as others with a different name and price tag. Become familiar with the products that you use and what chemical makeup they contain. If further questions arise, call the customer service department of the manufacturer and ask your questions. Look at the label and compare the different strengths. Some products are weak and advertised as adhancers.

Usually a stronger dose of sanitizer can achieve the same goal.

Sometimes it can be a contradiction of terms if a pool professional owns a retail pool supply store and also performs service. What I mean is that as a service tech, your job is to prevent, maintain, and cure using the best and most cost effective way that you can. In a retail environment, the key to profits is to sell products. Not to say that one would sell a customer something that he or she did not need, but you do have to sell a certain amount to pay the rent. Balancing this area is critical. If you take care of your retail customers as well as you take care of your service customers, word of mouth will increase your business. I tell you this by an example.

I know a person who owns a retail store and has service people do service on his customers' pools. His cure for everything concerning pool problems is sodium bromide sold as Yellow Treat. The product is good for what it was designed for, but it does eat up chlorine. This is the point. He sells more liquid chlorine that anybody in his area. Not only do his customers' pools have a demand for chlorine, but they are unstable because so much bromine is in their pool. A poor decision for customers but a great business plan. They have to add chlorine to activate the bromine and then shock it a couple of times to burn it out. It does not take a long time until the water becomes hard to manage. If this has happened to a pool you service or if the owner has added a lot of this product, draining some and adding new water will help lower the bromine level to allow the pool become more stable.

CHAPTER 6

Pool Problems

ALGAE INTRODUCTION

This is the fun part of this business for me. It is so much fun to take a pool that looks like a swamp and make it into a sparkling, clear, inviting place to enjoy. The look on children's faces when they see that their frog hatchery is now turned into this great place to cool off and spend the summer makes the work very satisfying. It makes everything that is unpleasant about this business worth the long hours.

There are many different forms of algae. Last count was over 20,000 different species. (And people say that this business is not a science!) They are broken down for us in four major categories: green algae, yellow or mustard algae, black algae, and pink algae.

GREEN ALGAE

Green algae are the most diverse group of algae, with more than 7,000 species growing in a variety of habitats. It is a paraphyletic group because it excludes the Plantae, which is plants, mosses, ferns, and flowering plants. Like plants, green algae contain two forms of chlorophyll, which they use to capture light energy to fuel the manufacture of sugars, but unlike plants they are primarily aquatic.

Green Algae, resembles its name by being green in color and is slimy on the walls and floors of pools. They usually form right at sunrise on the shaded part of the pool in the areas that I call the dead spots. These are areas where circulation is poor and hard to get to with the average brush. It is dangerous if it is in fiberglass or vinyl pools, due to being really slick and the chance of slipping and falling is very likely. Usually by brushing and by superchlorination, the algae will die. This form of algae can take over a pool overnight if left untreated. This is the fight against Mother Nature. You need to be at the top of your game and be aggressive.

I believe that working on problems in a pool is like being a veterinarian. The patient cannot tell you what is wrong, so all you can do is to treat the symptoms aggressively. Time on the job will help you with these problems.

On new pools where the surface is still curing (it can take up to 18 months to cure), for the first year prevention is a priority. In some cases, shocking a pool can force metals in the water to cling to the walls and cause staining. Older cured pools can withstand much more abuse than a new surface, so keep that in mind.

YELLOW OR MUSTARD ALGAE

Yellow algae, which I call wall clinging algae and mustard algae, are usually found on the shady side of the pool first. They have been described as sheet forming, and sometimes they are hard to tackle. If not attacked aggressively, they can spread the entire season by what I call re-blooming. Re-blooming or re-infection is quite common and is resistant to normal chlorine levels so that you have to hit the infestation hard.

Sodium bromide, sometimes referred to as Yellow Treat, is a good tool if the algae are just starting. If it is a reccurrence, it is time for major aggressive measures. The problem with bromide is that it eats up chlorine and causes problems with salt generators, a later topic.

Again, this is my personal, professional belief. If yellow algae recur within a couple of weeks of the first treatment, the real warriors are brought out. I believe that if yellow algae recur so quickly, something is causing re-contamination, or a re-bloom is active.

You know that normal cleaning is not performed on the insides of pipes, inside the niche of the light, underneath tiles, or in any other place where water may have gone. Yellow algae usually have a slimy protective coating and removal of it by brushing will help chlorine to kill the villain, but when you keep having this problem it is time to get mean and aggressive.

Sometimes proper treatment is not the option of the pool owner. In almost every case, it would be less expensive to use the good stuff than to brush until the brush loses its bristles. Stress this to your pool owner, and let him or her know that yellow algae attack on the walls of his or her pool and surface damage could occur and ruin the pool finish. Time is of the essence.

If I encounter a pool that has a re-blooming with yellow algae, I go for the big guns: the metals. The best metal algaecides are copper and silver. They do cost more, but they are cheaper in the long run. Silver is preferred, especially if there is a salt generating machine. Generally, a good silver algaecide will clear a bad infestation of yellow algae overnight if you have balanced the water to the manufacturer's suggestions on their product, so that it will work at its most aggressive manner. Copper has more chance for staining if not used right and is better for dark colored pools than for a light surface. Copper is also good in vinyl and fiberglass pools.

BLACK ALGAE

Black algae are very chlorine resistant. Having it occur in a pool with a good chlorine residue can happen and may not be the fault of anyone. Again: FILTRATION, FILTRATION, FILTRATION. Proper filtration will help prevent the formation of algae as well as proper circulation.

Many people want to fire the pool man when they get black algae. Some pools that keep a 5.0 chlorine level in a salt pool, with a good balance of water, with phosphates being regularly checked and treated, still have little black dots of algae about the size of a pencil eraser. If they do not disappear with the vacuum or Hammerhead, the stainless steel brush is the next weapon to use. If you brush the spot and notice a little puff of dust rise from the spot, it is probably black algae. If the spot brushes off easily, it might be time to give the pool a little shock—maybe more for my benefit than the pools'—but I do not get too excited if they brush up so that the FILTER can take out the algae particles. I usually brush them toward the main drain. If they remain after brushing it is time to raise the level of aggression, and I get that concerned feeling in my gut. I don't want to see a surface get damaged by algae. You have to keep in mind that it may not be your pool, but if you are maintaining it, it is your responsibility.

Black algae (blue-green) usually start as these little black spots. For you folks who prefer not to brush the walls and floor of your pool on occasion, there are things that are waiting to attack your pool. Brushing is also a preventive for algae, but will not prevent it altogether.

Black algae will form a layered structure where the top layer protects the lower layers. Remember Mother Nature. She protects herself. This alga is basically the same as you get on the grout line and right at the edge of your caulking in the corners of the shower. If left untreated, it can spread, and spread it will! It is slow growing but very hardy.

As algae consume carbon dioxide, which helps pH stay down, then the pH rises. Remember the story about pH at 7.2 the chlorine works at 80 percent and at a PH of 7.8 the chlorine works at 20 percent. As the pH rises, the effectiveness of your sanitizer decreases. Algae are different from the bacteria in a pool. Most bacteria take in oxygen and release carbon dioxide, but algae take in carbon dioxide that the bacteria has left behind and use it to grow. One of the problems with algae growth is that it feeds off one another, and my belief is that when algae are in your pool, the bacteria are growing also. You need to treat both. An aggressive sanitizer regimen is called for along with aggressive algae treatment.

A few years ago, we got a notice from someone in the business who warned us of algae called cyanobacterium. This form of algae is also listed as bacteria. Cyanobacterium goes back 3.8 billion years. Why have we not heard of it before? At this point in my career, I bought a microscope and a book on different algae and tested every one aggressively. Cyanobacteria are now one of the largest and most important groups of bacteria on earth.

Now usually cyanobacteria were found in oceans and fresh water streams. Somehow Mother Nature got hold of it and provided us with what we were lacking. It can also be of a single cell or what is called a colony that can form filaments, sheets, or even hollow balls. Some filamentous colonies change into different cell types when nitrogen is present. And rain water brings nitrogen.

The reason I brought this up was that cyanobacteria are harmless to you. Here is the tricky part. Once you kill the algae, the bacteria can turn deadly to humans. Our warning was only for a season, and I have not heard of any more of this lately. I brought you this little bit of information so that when you treat forms of algae, keep your people out of the pool until you are convinced that the alga is gone, you have a good balance of water, and your sanitizer is adequate and doing its job.

I can go on with all kinds of lessons on biology, horticulture, and things that can relate to plant growth. What you need to know is if you get black algae and an aggressive sanitizer regimen does not stop the growth along with real aggressive brushing, by all means get aggressive and get rid of the problem. It can start slow, but if the conditions are right, it can totally cover a pool really in no time.

I once was called out to a pool that was painted, and the owner wanted to know why the paint was bubbling. I am not a paint expert, but I went to see what the problem was and found out that an investor had bought the home, did a little work, and resold it to the present owners. What he did was criminal. He had a good bloom of black algae. Instead of taking care of the problem, he painted the pool, but the paint did not stop the algae from growing. Remember, black algae take in carbon dioxide not oxygen. The release of oxygen, I am told, is why the paint was bubbling. To sand blast the surface to remove the paint and algae and resurface the pool and replace the tiles, cost these people more than $8,000. That was the price for eight years ago. Double that now.

Black algae of any form can be your worst nightmare if not dealt with right. Some people disagree with me on this but if the spots that start forming cannot be dealt with and spreading seems to be occurring, then by all means go for the guns. Remember, it costs you less in the long run if you get aggressive early and get rid of the problem. Your pool owner will love you for it.

PINK ALGAE

I had never encountered pink algae until I came to Florida. My first case was in an on-the-ground pool. There were little pink spots on the bottom of the pool. I had to go research this and I did just that. The next morning the pool owner called and said the dots were the size of quarters. I went out there, and she was right. There were round spots of pink all over the bottom of he pool. The spots were slimy and the water had a milky look.

Pink algae is not algae at all but a fungus called paecilomyces lilacimus. It causes slimy white, pink, or gray colonies. It is found in aquariums but rarely in pools. May you never encounter it.

United Chemicals has an Environmental Protection Agency (EPA) approved pink algae treatment product called PinkTreat. I have never used this product nor do I know the exact chemical makeup. I do know it has to be activated with chlorine.

Pink algae can be removed by brushing the slime and shocking the pool. If the filter is not cleaned really well, it can recur again and again. If you have a cartridge filter, I recommend that you replace the element, and if a sand filter, change the sand. Backwash a DE filter and you should not have a problem if the filter has been previously maintained.

CLOUDY POOLS

The filter is the most important part of the system and has a lot to do with a cloudy swimming pool. Murkiness can sometimes be caused by the pool pump not running long enough, the filter not working properly, or damage to a DE filter that causes DE to enter the pool.

High pH and alkalinity in a pool or spa can cloud water. Cloudiness in a spa can be caused by excessive things in the water so that it becomes saturated and has a high TDS. This one is easy. Just replace the small amount of water. In a pool, things are a little different because of the volume of water. If water is properly maintained and the filter is running long enough to circulate the entire amount of water in 8 to 10 hours and if everything is where it should be, you need to check the TDS. It may be that the water is so saturated that it has particles smaller than the filter can take out. Try what is called a clarifier. There are many different ones and some flock a pool, which will be dealt with in another chapter, but you want a true clarifier that even if you overdose, it does not flock the pool.

A clarifier simply makes small particles attract each other to form larger particles so that the filter can remove them. Usually products that contain alum can drop all the particles to the bottom of the pool, called flocking, and that is one of the last resorts in my opinion along with replacement of some water. Once a pool has been flocked, vacuuming the waste is recommended.

OTHER REASONS FOR CLOUDY POOLS CAN BE:

1. Introduction of chemicals which have not been dissolved
2. Algae dead or alive in pool
3. pH is too high
4. Pool water is saturated
5. Air entering the pool through returns
6. Filter not properly sized for pool
7. Pump not running long enough to filter enough
8. Metals in the water
9. Newly plastered pool still releasing plaster dust
10. Contaminants in the water: dirt, algaecides, chalk from painted surfaces
11. Stabilizer level too high
12. Low sanitizer levels
13. Tree pollen
14. Improper balance of the water
15. Phosphate contamination

PHOSPHATES

Phosphate is called a "pollutant" although it is used in soaps, detergents, shampoos, and even soda pop. Other phosphate sources include fertilizers, organic debris such as leaves and bark, and some pool chemicals. Phosphate pollution in lakes and streams is caused mainly by over-development, which causes extreme amounts of byproduct waste to end up in natural water systems.

Testing for phosphates should be done regularly to help you stay ahead of algae. It takes far less effort to prevent a problem that it does to correct one.

Most phosphates enter pool water in the form of tri-sodium phosphate. Algae cannot use these combined phosphates as a nutrient for growth. It is not until the compounds of phosphates are broken down in the water to a free ortho-phosphate that algae can begin to thrive.

Once ortho-phosphates are removed from the water, it is harder for algae to thrive because the food for the algae is not available until the phosphate compounds break down as a result of oxidation, hydrolysis, and enzymatic digestion. In other words, all phosphates end up as ortho-phosphate, which feeds algae.

It is believed that algae can grow at a level as low as 10 ppb (lake and stream water). In a sanitized environment, algae thrive at 500 ppb. The higher the phosphate level goes, the more the algae flourish and the more resistant they become.

When algae have been eliminated, the process of phosphate removal becomes crucial. As algae die off, it exudes free ortho-phosphates that could lead to further growth even in the presence of an algaecide. That means the free ortho-phosphates ooze out of the dying algae and can re-contaminate the pool water.

Removal of phosphates will not kill algae. You have to do that separately. The other thing that needs to be remembered is that many of the products that we use to remove and prevent metals in the pool contain phosphates along with some scale inhibitors and removers. A common ingredient is diphosphonic acid. "Phos" in this word is a clue. This is a perfect example of adding one chemical to a pool and affecting something else. You take the metals and scale out of a pool and leave phosphates that promote algae growth. You as a professional and a pool owner have to balance the problem. Do you settle for some stains created by metal and scale or do you treat that problem and then treat the phosphates?

Again, my opinion is that you treat the metals first to the extent that you want to achieve and then treat the phosphates. If you have a return of the metal, you need to put the pool on a regular maintenance program for metals. What this does is put phosphates back into your pool on a regular basis. Here is the balance. Do you want stains or algae? The best way is to keep the level of phosphates low. The level will be determined by your pool and the environment or location. Run your pump at a rate that will circulate the water properly and then make sure your filtration is working and is sized properly for the application of your pool. Your filtration, as I have mentioned many times before will aid you in the prevention of algae and if your pool is prone to this condition, you may even have to upgrade your filtration system. Pools that have metals and develop phosphate problems need a DE filter to counteract these problems properly. Since we are talking about microscopic cells, the smallest micron level of filtration needs to be used.

If a pool is properly maintained and the equipment is

functioning properly, these problems may occur only occasionally and are not a great concern. Mostly it deals with your source water. Phosphates can become airborne and cause problems, but metals are introduced by your water source or by some other means like your lawncare person spraying fertilizer in your pool, by metal objects dropped into the water, or the dissolving of metal equipment because of improper balance of the water. That's right. A person can create problems in a pool that create another problem by not taking care of the first one. It sounds complicated and requires thought and understanding.

NITRATES

Nitrates are nitrogen compounds that are everywhere naturally. They are in our soil and atmosphere. They consist of a single nitrogen atom combined with three oxygen atoms (NO_3). The most common form of nitrate is fertilizer. It is also found in human waste, rain, animal feces, and leaves, or other decaying plant life.

Nitrates increase the sanitizer demand in the water. The level of sanitizer in pool water will be depleted faster than if there are no nitrates. Therefore, you have to increase the amount of sanitizer to overcome nitrates. A level of 10 ppm will affect demand on a sanitizer. Nitrates are fertilizer for algae (as are phosphates). The treatment for removing nitrates is to drain water and replace with new water. Prevention is the second step.

Nitrates enter the water by clinging onto you, onto Fido, and from fertilizer in the air. A man with a blower on his back is the enemy of a pool owner.

It is recommended that nitrates be tested as well as phosphates whenever an algae bloom appears.

TRIHALOMETHANES

This is a term seldom used. Trihalomethanes (THM) is a byproduct of sanitation, primarily chlorine. It was first discovered in drinking water. The best way for a municipal water supply to get rid of sanitizer byproducts is to switch to ozone.

As with stabilizer, the government has done very poor studies on the byproducts of chlorine and what effects it has on the human body and on pool water. I recommend that you keep an eye on this new problem and report the findings of any studies that are done.

METAL CONTENT IN WATER AND CORROSION

A common problem is that the light rings turn black. This is usually caused by poor grounding, which is called electrolysis. It is defined as producing chemical changes by passage of an electric current through an electrolyte. What does that mean? Another more detailed definition is an electrochemical reaction causing a black stain normally found around metal fixtures or on the plaster. It is caused by two dissimilar metals being plumbed together or from an improper electrical grounding of pool equipment or lights. Electrolysis also means the decomposition of water and other inorganic compounds in aqueous solution by means of electricity. Chlorine generators use this principle to produce chlorine from salt in the water.

When water wants something, it will take it. Whenever you have the balance of water out of whack, things happen. If your pH, alkalinity, or even calcium is too low for a period of time, the water wants to neutralize itself and it does it by oxidizing metals.

If it is too acidic, pH is very corrosive and when chlorine or bromine is introduced, it multiplies. Low pH can eat up the surface, metal parts, and especially the heat exchangers in heaters. The surface is also easy prey to low alkalinity and calcium hardness.

PLASTER ETCHING

Pool etching is generally caused by low pH or low alkalinity. It can also be caused by low hardness in the water. Once it starts, you cannot reverse it, but you can aid in slowing the damage. Balanced water is the best prevention. Etching can also be caused by improper installation of the product. Improper mixing, application, and curing can also contribute to surface damage of the pool.

CHAPTER 7

Spas and Hot Tubs

Spas and hot tubs are not the same. The two are similar since both have hot water instead of cool or tepid pool water. Some hot tubs circulate and some do not. When water is warmed over a certain degree, balancing it takes on a different meaning.

Now my opinion of a hot tub is a shell, whether it is made out of wood, concrete products, fiberglass, or acrylic. It offers the options of circulating, filtering, and heating the water to a certain degree. Some hot tub manufacturers and dealers advertise their product as a spa, when it is really a hot tub. I believe that a true spa has some therapeutic advantage. If you want to sit in hot water, you can do it in your bathtub.

Some of the first hot tubs in the United States were made out of redwood. They were basically tubs that had hot water in them, and people gathered and sat with each other for a social event. They enjoyed the relaxation of hot water and the effects that it provides to sore muscles and tired bones. Some of the first hot tubs had to have water heated separately and hauled in and dumped into the tub. Later they were able to have their own heating devices. Sitting in hot water and having a drink or two was quite relaxing. Sometimes too relaxing. When you raise your body temperature while sitting in hot water, the effects of alcohol increase, and some people have died from the combination.

HOT TUB HISTORY

If you want some interesting reading, investigate the history of early hot tubs. One of the oldest known spas that was called a mineral bath is still in existence in Merano, Italy. It dates back 5,000 years. It is believed that the Egyptians had therapeutic baths as early as 2000 B.C. Evidence also shows that the King of Media had a spa in 600 B.C. Ancient spas were heated by putting large stones in a fire and adding them to water when they were hot.

The Greeks had hot baths around 500 B.C. that were built by volcanoes and by hot springs that let them use natural hot mineral water. It was easier than heating rocks. The Greeks and the Romans knew how to throw a party. They had large public hot tubs and some had buildings with private rooms and even steam rooms.

Back around 460-375 B.C. the "Founder of Medicine" Hippocrates used hot water tubs to treat rheumatism and jaundice, the first recorded use of hydrotherapy. It was so important to them that some leaders claimed that if a person could not swim, he or she was uneducated.

Now the word "spa" is Hungarian and first referred to the natural mineral springs. In Bath, England, the baths there were 120ºF. They have been used continuously since 800 B.C. Even Queen Elizabeth I used them. They could generate up to one million gallons of mineral water per day and contained over 30 elements including calcium, sulfur, potassium, and magnesium. It was surely some hard water. The water even had a slight radioactive reading.

Now as we know from watching all the older movies that the Japanese have used hot baths for centuries. Public bathing was a social event. The soldiers of World War II brought this technology back with them to the United States and here we are.

The technology was not totally new to the Americas. The Iroquois Indians used hot springs located in what later was called Saratoga Springs, NY. The old legends say that sometime after 1767, Sir William Johnson was cured of a strange illness and then as the word got out, George Washington and Alexander Hamilton used the facilities for curing their illnesses.

President Franklin D. Roosevelt had a home in Warm Springs, GA., that he called his "Little White House." He used the hot water therapy there to relieve the pain caused by polio. He later dedicated the facility to people who had disabilities.

In the United States, wooden hot tubs started to appear in the 1960s. They started very simply, with wooden oak barrels that had been used for aging whiskey and wine. The barrel idea was followed by the use of redwood. However, they leaked and were hard to sanitize. Since that time the world of hot tubs and spas has come about.

SPAS

A spa heats the water inside its shell, has pumps that circulate the water, and most have special nozzles and effects that make the experience very enjoyable and relaxing. Some are not very expensive and some are out of sight. I maintain a portable spa that cost $33,000. That is not a misprint: it is $33,000. It has numerous adjustable jets that provide different effects, a stereo system that most would love to have, and a large plasma television set that rises out of the rear of the spa for the participants' enjoyment. The only problem is that when you have the two pumps fired up on the high setting and the blower going, you cannot hear the TV. At close range, you cannot take in the full picture provided by the television because it is too big. The spa even has what I call "spitters." It has four features that have four holes each that squirt water in the air across to the other side of the spa. I do not know exactly what benefit that has for your body, but it looks impressive. Fiber-optic lighting is joined with the spitters and at night, it is a light show. Most spas have adjustable jets that supply different amounts of air and water volume that you can control while you are in the spa to get the desired effect.

See center insert, photo thirteen – spa with television

Spas can be made of different materials. Concrete spas usually just circulate water and most have what we call a blower, a motor that forces air into the spa either through special dual-purpose jets, or through separate holes that force the air into the spa agitating the water for a bubbling effect that is quite pleasing.

A spa can be put almost anywhere. It can be built as an extension to a pool, set on a deck or separate room, built inside a deck, buried in a hole, or inside a house in a bathroom. You can find them inside motel rooms; health fitness centers; locker rooms for schools, colleges, and professional athletes; private health spas, and just about anywhere. I even used one on the border of the New Mexico and Colorado line that was 150′ from the motel, and I had to run through the snow back to my room. It felt good when I was in the water but getting out was an adventure.

See center insert, photo fourteen – pool and spa combination

An outdoor spa combined with a pool normally has its own circulation pump separate from the pool, and its own heater. A spa that is part of a pool or is built higher than a pool can have a feature called an overflow that allows water to enter the spa from the pool pump, usually one or two returns, and has a small area that usually has marble on top that allows the water to overflow and give the waterfall effect. This also allows the spa to use the water from the pool so it can circulate all the time and provide the same sanitizer for both the pool and the spa. A spa usually has its own sanitizer device so that when the overflow is turned off, the spa is a totally separate piece of equipment that can take care of itself and not let the heated water out into the pool, if that is what you prefer. Most spa heaters are gas or propane fueled and are very expensive to heat a large pool. Different pool controls can incorporate automatic actuators so that when you turn on the spa function from either a remote control or a spa side-control mounted next to the spa, the actuator turns off the overflow function and allows the main drain from the spa to open and circulate the water only in the spa itself. I will get into these special functions later.

A portable spa usually has the better features as far as the aromatherapy, different controllable jets that perform many functions, and various seating positions. Just about anything that you can imagine can be installed in a portable spa. Being portable and just being a shell that has plumbing installed gives a manufacturer more options for additional plumbing that is needed to perform all of these functions. Pre-built fiberglass shells can be purchased with the plumbing already included that can be set in a hole in the ground or in a pre-built structure. The building of a spa and the different functions are only limited to the imagination of the designer and, of course, the availability of money. Some manufacturers do a great deal of testing to make sure that the functions they provide have a special purpose or effect. There are some that put a couple of things in it to make it look half-way impressive and call it therapy. Unknowing individuals can have a very disappointing experience when it is delivered and they climb into it.

We used to have spas on display that were all ready to go and if a customer was interested, he could get into the display model and feel the effects before buying it. If a dealer will not provide that for you, be concerned about what they are selling.

We could go into all the different types of hot tubs and spas and waste many trees in the process and not accomplish very much. If you are serious about purchasing a spa, do research, make sure you can inspect the same model in operation and if they will let you, try it out. Manufacturers' warranties are very important, too. If they are proud of what they are selling you, they will offer you a good warranty. A lot of companies offer a five- to ten-year warranty on the shell itself; that is, if they don't use the old cop out that if you have a problem with the shell it was the result of the chemicals that you used. But some offer very limited warranties on the pumps, heater, and other equipment that are the heart of the system. Make sure they offer you at least one year if not more for them.

Before we get into the maintenance of a spa, we will get into some of the options that are available with them.

1. INSULATION. It is a very important part of a spa. It maintains the integrity of the temperature and as you know, the better the insulation, the less your electric bill will be. Looked at it carefully since the initial cost of the spa may be low, but without good insulation, your cost to operate it may be extreme.

2. OZONE. Ozone is a naturally occurring form of oxygen. It is a form of oxygen in which each molecule has three atoms instead of the normal two. Ozone occurs naturally in small amounts in the earth's stratosphere, where it absorbs ultraviolet radiation. Although it resembles oxygen in many respects, ozone is much more reactive. Because it can decolorize many substances, it is used commercially as a bleaching agent for organic compounds, as a strong germicide for sterilizing drinking water and to remove objectionable odors.

Ozone gas is extremely effective for controlling bacterial and viral contamination. It has been used throughout Europe for drinking water purification since the 1800s. The United States has just recently starting to use ozone and usually used chlorine to purify water. As you will learn, the water had to be maintained to ensure that the metal pipes were not being dissolved. Not only was chlorine used but also the pH factor had to be maintained.

After Europeans witnessed their soldiers being killed by chlorine gas from the Germans, they decided to find an alternative to chlorine as a drinking water sanitizer, and they developed ozone generators.

Ozone is manufactured in spas in two ways. Some ozonators, known as UV ozonators, use an Ultraviolet light bulb to create ozone. Others, known as CD ozonators use a safe electrical discharge passed through oxygen. The resulting mixture of oxone is injected into the water, and impurities are oxidized. The creation of ozone through this method is the most current and effective way of producing ozone in a spa.

Some ozonators emit a distinct smell. It is important to choose an ozone system with an "off-gassing" component. The best systems use ozone injectors, which push ozone into the water, and then agitate the mixture for optimal oxidation of unwanted particles and impurities. Next, the water/ozone mixture is pushed through an off-gassing chamber, where the ozone dissipates. This procedure allows ozone units to work constantly even while you're sitting in the spa—without the nuisance of ozone gas smell.

Because ozone acts as a powerful oxidant, it serves as a water purifier. This means that using ozone to clean your spa's water significantly reduces the amount of chemicals required to kill standing bacteria and impurities. Using an ozonator makes the water look crisp and clear.

I don't want to confuse anyone here but you will find that most spas do not come with an off-gassing system, just a light passing through a hose. This is what is called an ozone generator. The more expensive models will offer the CD version. Ozone does help in spas and if you have the choice of having it installed on yours, it is a good idea.

Ozone gas is very effective against bacteria and virus contaminations. The famous E.Coli bacteria can be killed by ozone. This shows you how powerful ozone is as a sanitizer.

3. FILTRATION. As you might have guessed, I could not leave this one out. Some spas have only one small cartridge filter. Spas that have a constant filtration system usually have two filters. One is used during the normal operation, which comes on from time to time to prevent the water from becoming stagnant and keeps the temperature level up to the setting. This too is found in the more expensive spas, but aids in the ability to use less electricity overall by keeping the water temperature at a constant level. The filters must be able to maintain the power of the pumps that the system uses. Some spas have multiple pumps that can go up to five horsepower. To achieve therapy, you need a large flow of water with moderate force.

The object is not to be blown out of the spa but to have enough force to give you a massaging effect.

4. BLOWERS. A blower has a motor and a fan that force air through the jets or preformed holes to give the spa a bubbling effect, intensifying the action of the water.

5. SPA PACK. A spa pack is the heart of the system. Inside the spa pack are the controls, which are now electronic boards and relays. Some come with gold contacts, which are recommended since they operate in hot and humid conditions that can cause problems for normal wiring and relays. The heater is usually inside the skid pack and resembles the same type of heater you find in your hot water heater. The controls are getting really sophisticated and can be programmed to do many different things. They also include safety limit devices that protect the spa and the bathers from overheating.

Newer spas come with a limit switch that stops the water temperature at 104°F degrees for safety. Some can be over ridden and some cannot be. This temperature and higher ones might cause a person to become very relaxed very quickly and this is primarily why the use of alcohol in a spa can be very dangerous. Many people have passed out in a hot spa and drowned. The spa pack attaches to the circulation pump(s) and is normally connected by unions, that unscrew by hand to let you service it easily without having to cut the plumbing.

One of the most important things in a spa is the electrical connection. It MUST have a ground fault interrupter (GFI) to prevent electrocution. Some of the more expensive and newer skid packs have their own, but the initial feed line for the spa must have its own. This is an area where a professional needs to do the job. It has to be properly grounded so that when you reach into the spa to get a water sample, you aren't fried. On the smaller, less expensive spas or hot tubs that are 120 volts, a GFI is also required for the plug that will supply the voltage to the spa.

The problem with balancing the water in a spa is that it is such a small volume of water that it takes very little to change the chemistry. You can actually turn the spa on and depending on what you add after a few minutes with the aggressive agitation of the water, you can retest it to see if it is in balance or has gone over. It is always easier to add a little more of something than to take it away; be patient and careful when treating a spa.

I have had some say that the sanitizer level and pH are the only things you need to worry about in a spa. That is false. Akalinity and calcium levels should be maintained to the manufacturers' recommendations to protect the surface of the spa. Alkalinity and pH levels must be maintained because of the small amount of water that goes through the heater and pumps. If water is corrosive, it does not take long to start dissolving the metal parts.

This is one of those areas that require some math skills because you have to change quantities and be able to calculate the EXACT amount of product that you need. Knowing the EXACT volume of water is especially important. Refer to the manufacturers' specifications for this and if you maintain a spa for a customer, you should have a copy of the manual on that spa for reference and proper operation. If the owner does not have one, either get it on the Internet, or have a copy sent to you from the manufacturer. They normally will not give you a hassle if you ask for one because the better the spa is maintained, the less they have to worry about a warranty situation, and if it is properly maintained, word of mouth from the owner will help them sell more spas. Word of mouth is key in this business.

I have all my spas, except one, on bromine. That spa is used by two teenage girls who occasionally break out with cases of acne after bathing in bromine water. You can use chlorine or some other alternative, but bromine withstands heat before it breaks down better than most. If they have an ozonator of some sort, the amount of sanitizer can be lowered depending on bather load and who uses it. Remember children using a spa can contaminate it by urinating in the spa really fast. I shock all my spas once a week with potassium monopersulfate. This product has gone by the name of Shock and Swim because you can use the pool or spa 15 minutes after putting it in the water. It is a nonchlorine chemical that will break up chloramines and bromines. Potassium Monopersulfate does not bleach surfaces or dissolve metals. It is the safest way to shock a spa using a chlorine or bromine sanitizer.

Due to the small volume of water in a spa when the water seems to be unmanageable or is cloudy or has a lot of saturation from lotions and makeup, simply drain it. The length of time between draining depends on many things, and it is up to you to determine when it should be drained. When you drain a spa, you need to get inside and clean the surface with a sponge. No harsh abrasives or chemicals can be used on a spa. If you have metal deposits, using a solution of citric acid and water will remove them. If metal is present in the water, soak your filters in citric acid and it takes just a few minutes to remove the metal deposits. Different manufacturers make solutions that clean the surfaces of the spa and headrests and are recommended as the products of choice. Do not use muriatic or any other acid on a soft hot tub or a fiberglass or acrylic spa. You could damage the surface and repair is expensive. That is the reason I recommend that you to have a manual for the spa on hand for reference.

Now bromine is very aggressive toward metals and that is one reason why you need to monitor the level correctly. It also can irritate the skin, eyes, and can cause a reaction to some people who have breathing problems. It also has an odor that I do not like. The word was derived from a Greek word "bromos" which means "smell." When you first open the cover of a spa that is on bromine, you will see what I mean. I always hold my breath on the initial opening. The pH of bromine is not consistent either. As discussed in Chapter 5, when bromine is introduced in water it forms hypobromous acid. The resulting pH depends on the level of this acid. So make sure you test your pH regularly.

Another good piece of advice is that on spas that are not made of concrete products, do not use liquid acid to adjust the pH or alkalinity. A drop of acid on a fiberglass or acrylic surface can blister or do other damage. Use of a dry acid is recommended.

The basic adjustments for a spa are in the chart section, but again I stress, you need to know the exact volume of water to do the job right.

Now if you are using bromine as a sanitizer, it is a good idea when you have filled the spa to establish a bromine bank of ions. To do this simply take two ounces of sodium bromide and two ounces of potassium monopersulfate and introduce them into the spa up to 500 gallons of water. The latter activates the bromine, and you have a bank of bromine ions that are working almost immediately.

I can guarantee you that if you goof, it will be noticed by the owner who will not be happy with you. That is why we charge as much for spa maintenance as we do for an average size pool. Take your time and make sure everything is right. Average treatment and testing and retesting can run an average of 45 minutes to an hour if you wait for circulation to mix your chemicals so you can retest. Do not hurry the process and be precise.

For those people who are mechanically inclined and are used to working with electricity and plumbing, spas can be a good source of income. Since they are running at a high temperature and using corrosive chemicals, repairs are needed from time to time. Always shut off the main circuit breaker to a spa when you do any service function including draining the spa. I do not trust circuit breakers or markings on the breaker panel so I always test for current before performing any service functions on a spa. It only takes a couple of minutes, and I know I will be going home after the service and not fried in someone's back yard. Every time I get into a hurry and do something stupid, I get shocked. Let me tell you that 220 volts hurts. It also does not take much to kill a person. A little bit of knowledge for you is that volts do not kill, amps kill. One amp delivered just right can kill a human. Do not become a statistic.

Concrete spas that are in combination with a pool are usually maintained with the pool water, but they can be a totally separate system that has no link to the pool at all. The following pool/spa combination has three pumps. One is a circulation pump for the pool. It has no additional return for the spa to create an overflow. The spa overflow has a separate pump that shares the skimmer line to supply water to this pump to put water into the spa to create the overflow needed to make the water pour over the marble ledge. It has a third pump that just circulates the spa water by itself and can be heated or used as a separate unit.

PROBLEMS OF HOT WATER

Now as temperature rises in water, bacteria thrive. What is more important is viruses also like the heat. Other things such as fungi exist in hot water. When a person sits in a hot tub and enjoys the water, other things start to happen. When vapor rises off the water, it contain spores of fecal matter, skin, and anything else that comes off a bather. This is a problem with public spas and pools. An inside spa creates additional problems. Without the fresh airflow, these spores cannot be blown away.

When the jets of a hot tub or spa are turned off, bacteria, scum, and fungi that are left in the piping or if it drains back from the filters, come into the water in great quantities. When you turn the spa on again you get a large amount of this unwanted debris rushing out of the pipes and what does not enter your body through your pores enters your lungs. Hot water opens the pores of your skin and allows the foreign matter to enter your body. When the jets of a hot tub or spa are running, they create a mist. This mist is what enters your lungs.

The manufacturers of hot tubs and spas argue all these points because this can limit their sales. We all know that money is more important than our health. I am not trying to keep anyone from buying a spa or hot tub, but I want you to be aware of what can happen if improper maintenance and chemistry of hot water are not followed.

Another example occurred in 1999 in the Netherlands. A hot tub on display at a flower show contained Legion Ella. It is a member of SARS which stands for Severe Acute Respiratory Syndrome. Legion Ella can lead to pneumonia. This disease made more than 240 people ill, and 28 died. A public bath in Japan was the source of 14 infections of Legionnaires Disease and one person died.

Being "safe" it not only applies to the handling of chemicals but to the proper sanitation of water. If you have a hot tub or spa or plan to get one, make sure you are dedicated to performing the task of maintaining it properly. Only takes a few minutes every day to have safe water.

A new bug called the hot-tub lung disease was recently discovered. It is Mycobacterium Avium. The EPA has recently recognized this as a big problem. In the past, they were concerned with giardia and cryptosporidium, as well as other viruses.

Chlorine does not have the effectiveness in hot water to kill these unwanted creatures since its effectiveness stops at 85°F. An alternative sanitizer is recommended. Bromine would be a good sanitizer with the addition of ozone.

Now sometimes we hear someone bragging about having their own personal spa in their bathroom. These are whirlpool baths or jetted bathtubs. Some of them work really well. They usually have fairly good force of water but being the size they are for one person the theraputic effect is limited. It always seems that the jet blows away from where you need it. Most have jets on the side of the tub and not the back or front. They do circulate water at a temperature that the bather wants so they are not bad by any means.

The problem is that a whirlpool bath has no filter. When soap products are introduced, as well as the other organic byproducts, the whirlpool will produce bubbles from soap and contaminants that have become entrapped in the whirlpool system. The tub drain actually only drains the water from the tub and not from the plumbing. So whatever was left in the lines and pump of the tub will be there waiting for you the next time you choose to use it. Using a foaming reducer as you would in spas helps deal with this problem.

The chemistry of the water in the spa is more critical to me than in a pool. With such a small volume of water it is more important that the balance is correct.

Newer spas have come a long way from the first ones made. Options that are available are almost unlimited. Spas can have single or multiple pumps depending on the options you have installed. Most spas have adjustable jets and air controls. They have many different sitting positions and controls designed to perform a therapeutic function. They are so advanced that, like computers, you need a child to operate them. Some incorporate aromatherapy, chromotherapy lighting, hydrotherapy, jet therapy, and about any other therapy for whatever ailment.

For therapy, the best exercise pool is one that forces you to burn some calories. There may be other manufacturers of this type of pool I refer to, but I know of only this one. It is a small 8′ x 15′ pool called the Endless Pool. It is a counter-current swimming machine. It functions by creating a current of water that is adjustable, and you can swim all day long and go nowhere. The best part of this pool is that it can be placed anywhere. It can go outside, inside, in a garage, a basement, or anywhere you have space. It also controls temperature. It has a very thick vinyl liner that is 28 mil and a 5.5 kilowatt heater. Olympic swimmers use these pools for exercising.

The great thing about this little pool is that you can almost build it anyway you want it. It can have many different covers from just a simple cover that retains heat and limits evaporation to automatic covers for security. The basic size can be adjusted to fit your needs. Some have hydrotherapy jets, mirrors so you can see your swim stroke, and meters. These meters measure heart rate, speed, distance, and time. They have underwater cameras so you can see your stroke and form. They have optional gas heaters, and you can even get one with an underwater treadmill.

If someone would like to exercise in water, but cannot have a regular pool, this pool is an excellent consideration. The company even has a unit that fits into a real pool. It fits into most existing pools so that instead of swimming a few strokes and reaching the end of your pool, you can swim for hours and never move an inch. It is a perfect product for the individual who likes to swim laps in a pool but does not have access to a large pool.

A spa needs a cover. The heat from the water will rise and the temperature will go down unless it is kept inside the tub. They have the basic solar cover, a full cover, and also a safety cover that can be walked on. A spa must be as child proof as a pool. Since portable spas usually are on a deck or screened room, they are easy for children to get into. The cover must be designed so that a small child cannot open it and get into the water. The best way to ensure safety is to have the spa located where the area can be locked up limiting access to the spa as well as having a cover. Most have heavy and hard-to-move steps, designed so that they do not move when you get in or out of the spa. Therefore, you have to make the spa inaccessable to the child.

Covers that are of the solid type usually have straps with latches that can be mounted to the spa's exterior so that each latch or clasp has to be unlocked to open the spa. If children are present or have access to the spa, it is your responsibility to inform the owner of the dangers and liability of an unsafe condition. As the professional, you should always look out for your clients' well being. If the client refuses to put safety measures in place, have them sign a release that protects you from any liability if anything happens. You may be terminated but you could also be sued if someone gets injured or killed. Remember that we are in the fun business. If a job site is dangerous to people, it is not a good place to hang your shingle.

The spa business is very lucrative for maintenance and service. The temperature of the water and humid conditions the equipment is located in make spas a repair waiting to happen. Since most manufacturers are located far away from most of the customers, service technicians are needed and welcome. Being able to advertise that there are local service people in the area where a potential spa owner lives helps secure the sale of spas. Service is as important as the equipment itself. Spa factories are a good place to get leads on customers. Some day the warranty will run out on their spa and they will require a service person to make repairs.

Word of mouth is how this business works.

If an individual understands how a spa works and has the ability to work on them well, building custom spas can be a very good source of income. Everything from the shells to all the equipment used in a spa can be found and purchased easily. Building one just requires the knowhow. I know a couple of people who make a good living doing this. A customer can usually get a better quality spa for the money if built by an independent than if purchased from a store. As with retail sales, everyone who touches a product has to have profit built in and that is why the costs are higher. We built a couple of spas and did very well with them, but you have to stand behind your work and equipment.

CHAPTER 8

Advanced Features and Equipment

CHLORINE GENERATORS

Many companies are in the business of manufacturing chlorine generators with many different options and functions, but the primary function is to produce chlorine. They do this by passing a mild salt solution in water through an electronic cell that converts the salt water into chlorine. When the chlorine dissipates, it turns back into salt. The amount of salt needed is about one teaspoon to a gallon of water.

Advantages of this system are that you will not have to carry heavy jugs of liquid chlorine around or buy expensive granular chlorines. Salt is inexpensive. The amount of salt used in a pool is far less than in the ocean and most people do not even know that there is salt in the water. The chlorine it produces is what I call "softer" than normal chlorine and leaves no residue. We can run higher levels of chlorine in a pool with no complaints of beaching clothes and irritation or discoloring of hair. Doing so results in better water sanitation of the above the limits that you would use in a tablet chlorination system. One reason for this is that you add the cyanuric acid (stabilizer) to the pool and the chlorine generator does not add to the ppm of stabilizer as a tablet feeder would that uses trichlor. In the long run, it will cost you less and save you time to use this system instead of the other means of sanitation.

The disadvantages are that the chlorine produced by the chlorine generator has a higher pH level and must be maintained on a regular basis. Also, a homeowner cannot cheat on trying to run the pool circulation pump on a shorter time since it requires a proper amount of time to produce a certain amount of chlorine. Therefore, the amount of chlorine produced daily by a chlorine generator can be regulated by two ways. One is the length of time the pump runs, and the cell, which is the electronic device that makes the chlorine, has time to produce chlorine. The other is how much of a percentage you require of the controls for production of chlorine. The best method is to run the pump long enough to turn over the water in the pool in eight to ten hours a day. Then you adjust the percentage to the desired amount of chlorine that you need to sanitize your pool. The higher the chlorine production, the higher the pH will be.

The other things that affect the chlorine generators are nitrates, phosphates, and bromine products. Each absorbs chlorine and sometimes absorbs the chlorine that is produced as fast as it is produced. Metals in the water can also cause problems and may even plate the cell with deposits. Copper algaecides are not recommended in a salt generated pool. Silver algaecides are not as damaging but should not be used as a regular maintenance when the pool is equipped with a chlorine generator.

It is recommended that you turn off the chlorine generator for the first couple of days after using a metal algaecide. It is also recommended that you turn the machine off whenever you add salt to let it dissolve well in the water. If we went back the next day to turn the salt generator back on after the addition of salt, it would not be cost effective. This is good for the pool owner, but not profitable for the professional.

Now since the electronic controls sense the salt level in the pool, some simply will not produce with a high salt reading that you get after the addition of salt into the pool. If you add too much salt, you either add water to dilute it or drain some out. Others will intermittently come on for chlorine production and then shut off, allowing some chlorine to be produced. It will sometime in this century burn the excessive salt off and then return to normal once the proper ranges are established. This is one of those areas that we have spoken of before: it is better to add a little and then add more later than to add too much.

The generators have built-in protection devices called flow sensors. The flow sensor tells the controls that you have adequate water flow to allow the control to send current to the cell for chlorine production. No flow means no chlorine.

Since the cells are restrictive, unwanted particles can attach themselves inside the cell and cause loss of production or damage. The main problems are mostly metals and scale. However, when you clean a cartridge filter and fail to drain the lower tank before removing the element, the junk that is floating around between the outside of the filter and the tank can pass through the return line right to the cell and clog it up. I have found many things inside a cell that I wonder how they got there. If it is unwanted debris, you can remove it by flushing the cell with water. Do not use a knife or metal object such as a screwdriver to do this. Damage will occur to the surface of the plates inside the cell and replacement can be expensive. I use a straw to aid in the removal of these items. If it is metals or scale, a solution of one part of muriatic acid to three parts of water will usually do the job. Stubborn scales may require a stronger solution but always refer to the manufacturers' recommendations on cleaning their cell. You will be glad you did. I just add the desired amount of water to a small diameter bucket that the cell can fit in and make sure that I unplug the cell from the control or turn off the power to the cell. I add the desired amount of acid and watch for bubbling or foaming. Remember, always add acid to water and never water to acid. When the cleaning action has stopped, remove the cell, rinse with clean water, and inspect. If you still see some scale, you may have to repeat with a little stronger solution of acid. Be patient because sometimes this may take a while.

Most machines have a preset time that tells you to inspect the cell. After you have inspected a certain pool a couple of times, you will know whether it is prone to having a build up or if you really need to inspect. Cells are usually hand tightened by a type of coupling and never should channel locks or any other type of tool be used to tighten the fittings. Lube the o-rings on the shoulders prior to re-installation to aid in the prevention of premature damage to the o-ring because of the chlorine in the system.

Problems that can occur with debris, scale, and metals in the cell are that they can give a false reading on salt concentration registered in ppm. They also can limit the production of chlorine and may even damage the cell beyond repair. I know of some systems that have been in the field for more than eight years and are still going strong because of having proper maintenance. They will treat you just the way you treat them.

Other than just producing chlorine, some of the more advanced systems can turn on the pump as well as other equipment at preset times and run them for preset times. They can also have safety devices to limit the time a certain function is allowed to run.

Example: a certain model has a spa and a pool function that allows the use of a separate spa that usually overflows into the pool to separate itself by turning actuator valves that cut off the water coming from the pool to the spa to create a fountain or overflow that resembles a water fall. When the spa mode is chosen, the spa functions separately and the chlorine production is limited to the amount of water that is in the spa. This action keeps the spa from over-chlorinating itself to a dangerous level for the user. It can also have a recurring preset time so that if the owner gets out of the spa and forgets to turn it back to the pool mode, it will do so on its own. Some can be programmed to run different times on different days of the week and perform different functions on those preset days. Depending on the unit, the functions are unlimited to what you can do.

If a professional or owner decides to have a unit installed to produce chlorine, one of the main things to look for is its warranty. Some are limited but the good ones have a really good warranty because the manufacturer knows it will last that long. Also, look for the technical help that you can get. Some of the systems we have in Florida have unlimited access to technical support even for the pool owner. Some manufacturers will not give you the time of day if you are not registered with them as one of their customers. These you stay away from.

Many things can affect performance other than the problems that I described earlier in the chapter. Some equipment is affected by power surges and close lightning strikes. Usually turning off the power to the unit and waiting for 30 to 60 seconds resets the system and clears up many problems. When the control gives you a strange problem that you have not encountered before, it is always helpful to reset the system first to see if that cures your problem. On a unit that has a problem that continues off and on for a while, you should talk with a technical person; it may even require inspection by an electrician for the answer.

All units are powered by low voltage to the circuit boards, and they cannot get wet. Water damage can cause many weird things to happen and some may clear up after drying and some may have permanent damage. Also, do not touch the boards with your hands and only use tools on them where you are supposed to.

I once had a TV repairman whom I called after I had tried to fix the TV myself. He told me that he would not try to repair his pool systems if I would not try to repair my TV. The moral of this story is if you do not know what you are doing with an electronic device or system, leave it alone. They are all powered by 115 or 230 volts initially which can light up your life if you touch the wrong thing. Also, the circuit boards are like a motherboard in a computer. Actually, that is what they are: small limited computer controls. Static electricity passing through your body looking for that perfect ground to match up with can destroy one of these circuit boards in a control box of a salt generation system. Only trained personnel should perform service on these systems.

Some units can do multiple functions. When choosing a system for yourself or for a customer, make sure it has enough functions built in to do the job needed, and it is a good idea to get a unit that has some additional functions rather than adding them to a pool later. It is also important to make sure that the normal operation of the system can handle the equipment that it is going to control. Some relays are limited to the amperage that they can supply. It may be that the main relay can only activate a one and a half horsepower pump motor, but you have a two-horsepower pump. Some units have additional relays that can handle the extra amperage. It all boils down to the fact that you have to know what you are buying to perform the task you expect the unit to perform. When you buy an electrical unit such as a salt generator and install it only to find out that it will not do what you want it to do, it is too late. It is yours and no one will take it back. Always consult with a professional or the manufacturer to determine the proper system for what you need to do the job efficiently. Most systems handle up to 40,000 gallons (151,400 liters). Pools larger than this may require additional cells or complete units.

See center insert, photo fifteen - finished and filled pool

I service an 86,000-gallon pool with two units turned up to 90 percent that provide me with more than a 5.0 ppm chlorine reading every week and only use about 100 pounds of salt per month. That is a very small percentage of money that a different type of chlorinating system would cost. In colder months we turn the units down, and in the summer we crank them up.

Most units also are equipped with temperature controls so that if the water falls to a certain temperature, they shut the chlorine production off. A general rule is that at a water temperature of 55 degrees, algae will not form and grow as long as it has not already been established. Since not too many people can deal with this low temperature of water or can survive being in the water at this temperature, sanitation usually is not required. Bacteria likes heat, not cold. If you did not know this, here is a little information from the pool industry. Most commercial refrigerators for the food industry are required to keep the temperature of food at 51 degrees. At this temperature bacteria cannot grow. When the temperature of food is raised to 165 degrees and held there for 15 seconds bacteria are killed. Anything in between these temperatures is fair game for bacteria. That is the reason that we have to sanitize pool water.

Some systems can be controlled from inside your home with a mounted or portable remote control. From the comfort of your couch, you can turn on your spa and heater and after a few minutes walk out and jump into a hot spa. You can activate water features such as waterfalls, spitters, or many other things by the push of a button.

See center insert, photo sixteen - pool, spa, and waterfall

For that perfect atmosphere you can turn on fiber-optic lighting or standard lighting before you go to your pool or spa. Here in Florida it is a good idea to see if any creatures are in the water before you hop in. Water moccasins, very poisonous snakes, do not like to share their water with humans. I personally like to inspect the water before entry because I see enough snakes curled up in skimmers during the day that I do not need to share my pool with one. A pool light at night will also show you how clear your water is.

An advantage to a salt generated pool from the service point of view is that you can determine whether you have a leak in the pool or spa by the salt level in the water and by the stabilizer level in the pool. Losing salt and stabilizer indicates a possible leak because those two components do not evaporate. The addition of water does dilute them to a certain extent but normally if there is a drop in those two areas and you have to add water, there is a leak. It is especially helpful on pools with an automatic water level device.

See center insert, photo seventeen - finished and filled pool

The automated controls are costly at first, but you do save money and comfort as time goes on. (Australians are one of the most advanced countries in pool sanitation and in the development of pool systems and controls. In many respects, they are the leaders in swimming pool technology.)

There are also controls that provide all these services that I have described but do not have a built-in salt generator system. They have remotes and receivers at control boxes that activate relays that activate different equipment. Most of the receivers have a button or switch that can also be operated by manual means to keeps you from having to dry off and go into the house to turn on a certain function of your pool system. While most remotes cannot get wet, they do make what is called a spa remote that can actually float in water and is waterproof. Some have limited functions and cannot do all that a wall mounted unit can.

Remotes bring up the subject of radio frequencies. What we

have experienced in certain subdivisions is that if two identical pool systems are close to each other, it is possible for a pool owner to push a button on his remote and activate a neighbor's system. Most systems have multiple frequencies that can be used to prevent this from happening if programmed properly. There are some that do not, so it is best to check it out before installation so a problem does not occur. It will only be a matter of time before the kids discover that they can grab the family remote and drive around town and harass pool owners.

CHAPTER 9

Automatic Cleaners

The different types of automatic pool cleaners are endless. Some work off the suction of the pool pump, and some are a pressure-feed system which has a separate pump called a booster pump for cleaners. Some clean a pool randomly and some have a pre-program that they follow and have a certain pattern that they perform.

Each cleaner is designed for a certain type of pool. Some will work only in vinyl pools, and some will work only in concrete pools. Some create suction by the use of a diaphragm that sucks the debris in while going around the bottom and the walls of the pool. Some have wheels and actually drive themselves around the pool sucking up the unwanted debris and stirring up substances on the bottom by spraying water from the rear of the cleaner or a tail to allow the debris to be pulled into either the main drain or skimmer and let the filter remove these items.

There are other cleaners that are electric powered and have a storage device or bag that lets them crawl around the pool and remove and store debris. All cleaners except for the diaphragm model have a separate storage system designed to remove unwanted debris. Most diaphragm models connect to a separate cleaner port installed in the pool or through the skimmer and on the skimmer models deposit the debris in the trap basket of the pump unless they have an inline leaf basket to collect larger pieces of debris.

The choice of cleaner depends on the suction power of the pump and the design of the pool it will serve. Some cleaners get stuck on stairs, ladders, and different shapes of certain pools. You have to do your research to determine which cleaner will work better on that particular pool.

When we had our retail stores, we had models of cleaners that we put in customers' pools for a trial basis to see if the cleaner could do the job properly. If for some reason a particular cleaner could not perform well in a certain pool, we tried another kind to get the best cleaning action possible. We concluded that if a pool had small amounts of debris or that the particles were fairly small, one type of cleaner might work. If the pool had a large amount of leaves in it, usually a pressure-fed cleaner worked better. Some electric powered cleaners actually shred leaves into smaller pieces for easy removal.

It all boils down to money. If you want the best cleaner for your pool, it costs. If you want it to do a fairly good job, it might cost you less. A cleaner that does not perform the way it was intended to do in your pool or a customer's pool is a waste of money. Experience is the key here. Manufacturers promise a lot of things that may not pertain to a particular pool. You have to know your product that you wish to sell and install and know it well. Selling and installing a cleaner that does not perform properly in a pool is a sure way to make a client mad. As with a lot of things in this business if you have doubts, contact the manufacturer. They prefer that their product works well and does not have a problem. A good rule of business is simply this:

your worst advertisement is a dissatisfied customer. It will be your fault that you sold them the product and not the fault of the product. Know your product well and how it works with different pool designs and systems and if you do not know them well simply do not recommend them. A bad decision can cost you more than one customer.

Usually a pool that has a screened enclosure is a fairly good candidate for a suction cleaners, depending on the design of the pool and what the pool has in it. Suction cleaners are not good for lots of leaves as they get plugged in the diaphragm of the cleaner disabling them. Anything that is in the pool that can clog the cleaner is bad for the cleaner, and it will not perform well. If a ping-pong table is near the pool, load it in your truck and haul it away. Ping-pong balls can do serious damage to either a cleaner or a suction line. If one gets sucked into a line and get plugged in a 90 degree fitting, it will be there until the end of the world. If a pool is plumbed with one and a half-inch plumbing, ping-pong balls can easily plug suction lines. If a two-inch line is used, you may be lucky enough that it passes to the pump. Let the pool owner know the dangers of ping-pong balls getting into the plumbing of pools.

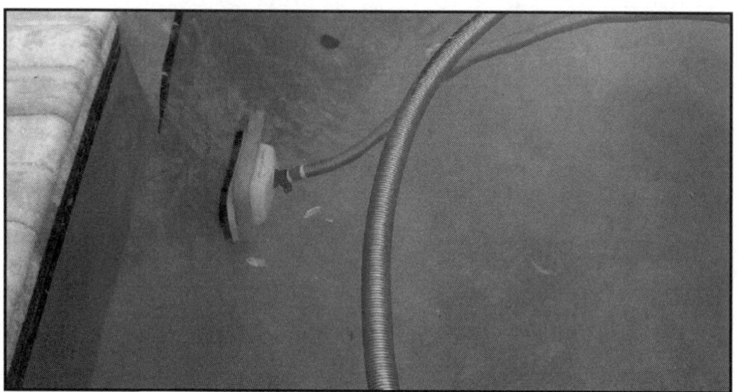

See center insert, photo eighteen – suction cleaner

In Florida there are many pine trees constantly dropping needles that with some leaves can clog a line that may not get unplugged and can give a cleaner a run for its money. Unlike your household sewer lines, it is dangerous to put a plumber's snake into a pool line. It is also recommended that high pressure air not be shot into a pool line. We can get into these problems later in the repair section.

A cleaner is designed to aid in the cleaning of a pool and not to replace the normal cleaning that is required. Tiles still need to be cleaned. Walls and floors still need to be swept, and a good vacuuming needs to be done. People need better education who think if they install a cleaner in their pool that they don't have to do anything else to maintain it. They should consider how long they want the pool surface to last. The average in this area is seven years. With good maintenance it can be longer, but relying on a cleaner by itself can shorten the lifespan and the beauty of a pool surface.

As for the pool owners' needing better education, a service person who installs a pool cleaner must give the pool owner proper instruction to deal with the cleaner and how certain suction lines may have to be adjusted to achieve a required suction to make the cleaner work properly. The owner needs to know that as the filter traps debris there is less water flow and less suction, meaning a less effective pool cleaner. Also as the suction is restricted so also is the amount of circulation that the pool experiences. Then the filter does not perform properly, leading to other problems such as algae and unwanted deposits on the walls and floors.

CHAPTER 10

Other Procedures

CLEANING SAND FILTERS

There are times when you might choose to clean a sand filter rather than change the sand in it. The procedure is very simple. If the filter is equipped with a removable top where the gauge and relief valve are located it is really simple. The first thing that you need to do is to backwash the filter very well. If it is equipped with a multi-port valve (a valve with several positions)—even better.

Always turn the pump off before you try to move the valve. Failure to do so will result in damage either to the filter or to you. The force of pressure that could be released because of moving the valve while the pump is running can literally blow the top of the valve off. When you stand in front of the filter to move the valve, look down and you will see that your face is directly above the handle. Think about what I just said and picture the top of the valve blowing upwards. You are in the pathway of a very dangerous item that consists mainly of CPVC and it shatters into pointed shards. Each movement of the handle on the multi-port valve must be done with the filter pump off.

If you have survived this far, I can assume that your head and face are still intact. After the initial backwash, where the liquid is coming out of the waste port of the valve and it is running clear, turn the pump off, change the indicator back to the filter position, and turn the pump on. Run it for a few seconds to loosen up debris that did not come loose the first time. Repeat this process until the pressure of the gauge does not drop anymore. It can take three or four times.

Put the filter valve in the closed position. Most sand filters have this feature on the multi-port valve. If they don't, here is how you can do this procedure. Once the valve is in the closed position, take that top I talked about earlier and remove it. Most are threaded and need to be unscrewed. The filter usually comes with a wrench designed to remove the top of the filter. If it does not, one should be purchased. Using channel lock pliers is not recommended but since we all have a few pairs of them, be really careful using them because you can damage the top very easily. Remove the top and pour a cleaner designed for sand filters in the top. You want to leave the pump turned off for the time that is recommended on the label of the product. It is highly recommended that you either disable the timer or turn the main breaker off for the filter pump. If you do not do so, you can damage equipment. After the recommended time expires, you can remove the drain plug in the bottom of the filter and let all the water out. Once all the water has drained from the filter re-install the plug and turn the valve to backwash. Install the top of the filter remembering to lube the o-rings with a non-petroleum lubricant designed for o-rings on pool equipment. Once the top is put back to the position where it is supposed to be, you can turn back on the circulation pump. Backwash the filter until the water runs clean. Repeat the backwash procedure a couple of times to be sure you have removed the most debris that you can.

If you do not have the closed position or you have a slide valve, do this: after backwashing until you feel that you have removed all the loose debris, remove the drain plug from the filter and let it drain completely out. After the water has drained from the filter and you have re-installed the drain plug, turn the filter valve to the filter position. If the top is off the filter, you can pour the product in the filter, or if you do not have a removable top, remove the filter pump trap lid and simply pour the product into the pump trap. Reinstall the lid and turn the pump on until you see that water is flowing to the pool, or if you have the top removed you can see water at the top of the level of the sand. The filters are not totally full of sand. When you are convinced that it is as full as it can get without releasing water back into the pool, shut the pump off. Perform the same procedure as far as giving time for the product to work and also disabling the pump. After the proper time has passed, backwash the filter to remove all the cleaning product residue, and then you can resume proper filtration of the pool. If the filter shows no sign of cleaning up, you have to change the sand in the filter. The rule of thumb for all filters is that your starting pressure (which is the pressure the gauge read when first installed and turned on), reaches 10 psi higher than the initial reading, it is time to backwash. On a sand filter the more debris that is in the filter, the better it filters. This is not true in a DE filter to that extent. Regular backwashing of a sand filter will help in filtering the pool to the best quality that it was designed for.

CHANGING SAND IN THE SAND FILTER

Here is the procedure for changing the sand in the sand filter. First, turn the pump off. Pull the plug on the filter and let all the water out of the tank. When all the water is removed, you need to unscrew the bolts holding the top part of the tank and carefully remove it. If the tank cannot be split, the lid on the top of the tank will come off. If the filter is equipped with a top mounted multi-port valve, you remove the valve. The sand has to be removed. You can either use a small container to remove a little sand at a time until it is mostly gone or you can use a shop vacuum to remove the sand. The laterals are located in the bottom of the sand filter . Take care when working around not to damage them. Most tubes on the laterals will fold up for easy removal. Make sure that you inspect the laterals for cracks or breaks, which would mean that they must be replaced.

When everything is clean and all the sand and debris have been removed from the filter, it is time to reassemble the filter and add the sand. Any o-rings that are on the filter should be replaced at this time to prevent leaks. First, replace the drain plug. Install the lateral assembly into the bottom of the filter. Fill the tank with water until it covers the laterals by a couple of inches, helping to prevent damage to the laterals when adding the sand because sand is very heavy. When adding the sand go very slowly until all the laterals are covered. Filters have a tool that holds the stand pipe straight up so that when you install the valve you do not have to force the stand pipe to put on the valve thus taking a chance on damaging the laterals and the lateral assembly. Do not get sand in the stand pipe or it will wind up in the pool and usually pass through the valve and damage the gaskets and o-rings. On most models that you can split the tank, the lateral assembly is held in place with the bulkhead fittings that screw into the pipes that are attached to the lateral assembly and the upper diffuser. These you can just leave in and work around. When you get the sand down to a good level, the laterals will fold up for inspection or you can remove the entire part and inspect. If you remove the bulkhead fittings, make sure you replace the o-rings that go between the bulkhead and the filter tank.

Let's talk about the sand. It is not play sand or sand that you find on the beach. It is a silica that is sized for proper filtration. Do not use sand that is not made and approved for the sand filter. Follow the manufacturer's recommendations.

This is a good time to check the multi-port valve gasket and upper valve assembly, usually called a cover, for damage to the shaft, non-metallic bearing, the spring that holds it down against the gasket, and the gasket itself. If the gasket is damaged, the filtration process can be limited and sand can go into the pool. A fairly good way to tell if you have a problem with the gasket is while the filter is operating in the filter position, look to see if water is leaking out of the waste port or see if you have sand in the bottom of the pool. These observations should be made before you tear the filter down so that you can inform the pool owner that there are more problems than just dirty sand.

Once all has been inspected and repaired and the sand is put back into the filter, the first order of business is to backwash the filter to get rid of impurities in the sand. If the multi-port valve has a rinse position on it, turn it to rinse. That position is designed to clean the pipes out. When that has occurred, you can turn the pump off and put the valve in the filtration position and turn the pump on. Open the relief valve so you get the trapped air out of the filter, and once that is done, look at the returns in the pool to see if you see any sand or debris going back into the pool indicating a problem. At this point, record the pressure on the gauge so that you know that when it gets 10 psi higher, it is time to backwash.

Sand filters that are used on pools with chlorine or bromine can go a couple of years without having to change the sand depending on bather load, trash that gets into the pool, and how well the pool is maintained. If the pool is on a nonchlorine sanitizer such as biguanicides, sand should be changed yearly.

CLEANING A CARTRIDGE FILTER

Cleaning a cartridge filter does not resemble cleaning a sand or DE filter. As described earlier the filter element resembles an air cleaner on a truck or tractor. Normal maintenance is that you spray the filter with a good nozzle to remove trapped particles between the pleats of the element. The same rule of thumb applies to a cartridge filter of 10 psi above the initial pressure: it is time to clean it.

At times you will find that once you have sprayed the element so that you think it is clean and installed it back into the filter body, you will notice that the pressure is still high. That means that the element either has oils and organic particles imbedded in it or has calcium or metals attached to the element media. If the deposits are organic materials or oils and suntan lotion, you can simply soak the element in a solution of dishwashing liquid that has enzymes. Filter cleaning solutions are on the market, but everyone who has a cartridge filter should have a spare filter and a bucket or a plastic trash can for continually soaking the spare element. A good cleaning takes 48 hours.

Once you soak the element in this solution make sure that you get all of the soap or cleaner out of the element. Let it dry completely and then pick it up. If the element is still heavy, that means you have other particles attached to it. If it is iron, you can soak the element in citric acid a few minutes, and that will remove the iron and rinse it off well. If it is calcium, you can soak it in a solution of three parts water to one part muriatic acid. If the element contains hard deposits, it will foam. Once the foaming stops, that means the job is done. Take the element out of the solution and rinse it well. Let it dry and once completely dried, the filter should weigh the same as it did when it was new. If cleaning cannot cure your problem, it may be time to replace the filter element with a new one.

Now when I discuss this procedure with other individuals who take care of pools, some of their answers are, "Why should I clean an element when I can replace it and make money off of the part?" A professional should always make the attempt to do the job right—in a manner that does not require that the owners must pay for things that they really don't need. All homeowners who have a cartridge filter should have their own trashcan, that lets them soak the element at their place. After all, a plastic trashcan and a bottle of dishwashing liquid is far cheaper than a new element. I have a set-up at my house where I do that for my customers that do not have a trashcan or do not want to have one in their yard. I deal with a lot of high-end properties and I can understand this. I can honestly say that it is for my benefit as well as theirs. On the job-site, it is quicker for me just to pull the element out and replace it with a clean one than to try and clean an element with no success. Improper water flow can result in problems that you will have to deal with later. Remember filtration cures and prevents a lot of problems.

CLEANING A DIATOMACEOUS EARTH (DE) FILTER

A DE filter is a different monster, and normal maintenance

should be done yearly to prevent problems. The best time to break down a DE filter is at the beginning of the swimming season so that it will last and treat you well during high use. If DE filters are properly maintained at regular intervals, you should have no problem if they are sized properly for the pool and the amount of trash the water collects. A screened-in pool has fewer problems than a pool exposed to the elements.

See center insert, photos nineteen and twenty – screened pool

There are many different types of DE filters. Some that are still in use are the old finger type called extended-cycle filters, meaning that when the pressure rises, you can actually "bump" the filter and knock the DE and the debris off of the fingers. The theory behind this is that the heavy debris will fall to the bottom, and the light-weight DE will re-attach to the fingers to filter the water properly. When this no longer works, you change the DE. When the pressure does not come down, you have to break the filter down and follow the same cleaning procedures as the cartridge filter: enzymes for the organic materials and acid for the hard stuff. When cleaning this type of filter, always replace the diaphragm gasket.

Cleaning is easier on the newer filters that have grids in them. Grids are usually long elements that are fabric-covered where the DE can attach itself and filter out particles. A DE filter can filter down to three to seven microns. When backwashing does not take care of the problem and you switch from filter to backwash a few times but the pressure still stays high, it is time to break it down. By the way, if you have a problem with a filter and you are not sure that the pressure is right, try a known good gauge to make sure it is a filter problem and not a gauge problem.

Most grid filters will come apart in the middle so the grids can be exposed. I always drain the filter with the drain plug in the bottom first and then remove the top. Once the top is removed, you can see what the problem is. If the DE is packed between the grids really hard, you can spray them off in the filter and try to remove as much of the DE and debris as you can by draining the water out of the drain hole. If you can totally clean the filter by this method, you may have done the trick. The problem that can occur with DE packed in between the grids is that they force pressure on the grids, and the plastic piece on the top of the grid that fits into the top collector manifold can break off and DE can leak back into the pool. With it plugged, you may not have that problem until you have cleaned the filter. It's a catch 22.

Before I remove the manifold and remove the grids, I perform another little check. I mix a solution of three parts water and one part muriatic acid in my water can that I use for acid washing pools. You must have all the DE off the grids or it will foam with just the junk on them. If you disperse a little of this solution on the grids and get a lot of foaming, you may need to clean the filter with acid. Most of the time taking the grids out and hosing them down will do the job. If for some reason there is a lot of organic material on the grids, you may have to soak the grids in enzymes. Most DE filters have only a four-position multi-port valve or a slide valve and do not have a closed position. What they do have is a boost position that closes the filter off, and you could add cleaner to the filter, but I have had little success with this since it requires spraying the grids well to get rid of all the DE.

Taking a grid filter apart is easy. Putting it back together requires patience. After you have the filter grids out, rinse them off so that they are as clean as they can be by this method. Once they are clean, spray water into the inside of the grid and see if the water drains. If it holds the water in, the filter grids are plugged and you have to do the same procedure as the cartridge filter as far as cleaning the grids. I would try to clean them with the water jug and acid method first. If you get a lot of foaming, you may have to rinse and reapply acid until it quits foaming. Once the grid is rinsed, put water back into the grid and see if there is any improvement. You can tell by performing the task on a single grid and if it works, you can do the rest.

Most filters have what is called a short element mixed in with seven full elements. They have to go back the way they came out to avoid putting the grids in stress. You can damage a grid if you do not get it put back in correctly. In the bottom of the filter where the grids sit is a plate that has slots called a locator. The grids have to be placed perfectly in the locator to prevent damage. When you think you have it mastered, you have to install the top collector manifold and those slots in the grids have to fit in the manifold where they have plastic key ways that lock the grids in so they do not move. This is where even more patience is necessary. I have had them fall into place, and I have had the filter that does not want to cooperate. You have to work each grid in separately and be gentle. Do not force anything together.

There is usually a standpipe that has an o-ring on it, and it should be replaced. Always lube the o-rings. The standpipe acts as a support for the top collector. You start the collector on the standpipe, slowly and carefully push it down until all the grids fit as they are supposed to. When you tighten the manifold, just snug is all you need. Plastic parts do not take much force. Check carefully before tightening the nut holding down the collector that all the grids are in the proper position. When you have tightened the nut holding the manifold, apply a layer of silicone around the threads of the bolt that comes up through the center of the manifold so that the threads do not get damaged or rust to make it possible to take it apart the next time.

After you have assembled the grids, it is time to put the top back on. Most DE filters have a very large o-ring around the bottom of the tank. Usually you can re-use this o-ring if you clean and lube it really well. Install the top back on and secure it properly. Now you can re-install the drain plug, make sure the valve is in the filter position, and turn the pump on. After you have bled the air out of the filter and the pressure looks normal, inspect for leaks. If none are found, add the proper amount of DE for that filter in the skimmer slowly until the skimmer has sucked it all down. The object is to put all the DE into the skimmer and none into the pool. DE will settle on the bottom of the pool and will make a mess if you let it get into the water. When that task is complete, check for leaks again and you are finished if the pressure has come back to normal. I have always been able to clean grids on a DE filter successfully and only had to replace them when they are damaged and leaked DE back to the pool.

DRAINING THE POOL

Draining a pool is fairly simple but there are some precautions to consider. If you have a high water table, draining a pool can be dangerous. If the water pressure under the pool is high, the pool can literally pop out of the ground. This is especially true with a fiberglass pool. A vinyl pool should never be drained all the way, whether it is on-the-ground or inground. I will get into that later.

A good circulation pump may drain much of the water out of the pool, depending on the location of the pump. If the pump is higher than the pool or a long distance away from the pool, it may hesitate as the level goes down. If using the pool pump to lower the water level, you have to shut the skimmers off either by using a valve or by putting a plug in the skimmers so they do not suck air. This also applies to cleaning ports in the pool if they are dedicated to a suction type cleaner. Once you start, do not stop the pump. It may not be able to pick up a prime with a lower level of water.

A good submersible pump is used to get all the water out. They make those that fit inside a main drain so you remove all the water. They are used when you acid wash a pool. They simply attach to a vacuum hose and if you need to locate the water farther away, the hose is long; then you can attach backwash hose to the vacuum hose and extend it out to wherever you want it. You might check with local codes on pool draining. Requirements are different in different areas. It usually is a violation to drain pool water into a stream, lake, or some sewer systems. Always check first to make sure you are not violating a code or law.

Now for the safety of the pool, drain it, make the repair, and refill it as fast as is possible. If you think you have a high water table and have to leave the pool for an extended time, remove the plug at the bottom of the drain to relieve some pressure. If water comes in through the plug hole, you need to work quickly, replace the plug, and fill the pool. I don't leave a pool drained overnight if I can help it. Here in Florida it can be a disaster. You can check with your local pool builders to see whether they have had a problem in a certain area with high water tables. The other way is to dig a hole with posthole diggers or have one drilled to the depth of the pool to see if you have water filling in the hole you have dug. It is always best to drain a pool when the rainy season is over or surface water is not present. You will have to be the judge of this but always use caution. An accident could cost thousands of dollars.

Now for personal safety when using a submersible pump, make sure the plug that you use has a Ground Fault Interrupter (GFI).

Disable all pool equipment by turning off all the breakers in the service panel that have anything to do with anything that goes to the pool. Electricity and water do not mix well. Safety first is a prime concern. Pool technicians as well as pool owners have been killed by not being safe. If you are in a pool with a pump and you feel that strange tingling that makes you think of a mild shock, get out of the pool and check the equipment. Do not go back in until a professional electrician checks the home power supply. This must be taken very seriously. Pool technicians who do things on a repeat basis sometimes play loose with the safety issues. It only takes once to be dead.

Now if you drain the pool and have removed the plug in the bottom of the drain, remember to re-install it properly before filling. Forgetting happens many times across the country, but normal people usually only do it once.

The goal that one tries to achieve is to drain the pool early so that you have plenty of time to do the job you intend to do, and then have it filling by nightfall so the pool does not have to sit empty overnight. Whether you start at 4 a.m. or use multiple pumps, get the water out, do the job, and start putting water back in to keep the surface from drying out. When the water is removed, do your best to keep the surfaces moist so that they do not dry out totally.

ACID WASHING A POOL

Acid washing is used to remove build up on the walls and floors of a pool or spa. The buildup can be excess plaster, scale deposits, minerals, metals, and some chemical residue. Acid washing eats away the build-up and can etch the pool if left on too long. It will not make repairs from rough installation of the surface nor is it a miracle cure for dye streaks that leach out of the surface. If the surface is coated with dirt and different oily substances, they have to be cleaned first. An acid wash will not kill algae, and algae have to be killed and removed first.

Let me talk about the safety issues first. Acid is dangerous to use. It can kill you if things go wrong. One of the worst situations happens if you use a chlorine product to kill algae anywhere in the pool and you put acid on top of that; you have just made your own gas chamber. If you use a sanitizer to clean and kill algae first, you must rinse the pool surface down very well and let it air dry. At this point, it is highly recommended that you use a respirator to keep the poisonous fumes from entering your lungs. In fact, it is highly recommended to use a respirator anytime you acid wash a pool. These chemicals can react with many different things and can overtake a person so fast you cannot escape a pool.

Now if I acid wash a pool that has algae, I usually use a mixture of granular trichlor or dichlor diluted in water. I scrub the surface with a wire brush to clean algae off the surface and let the chlorine do its job. This may not take very long. It depends on the type of algae. The best way to acid wash a pool that has algae is to clean the algae first and then drain the pool. If time is important, I recommend this. Forty-eight hours before you drain the pool, treat it with silver algaecide. Scrub the infected areas well with a stainless steel brush to break the protective barrier of the algae. Let the pump run the entire time until you show up to drain the pool. What this does is very simple. It will kill the algae on the surface, but more important, it will kill the algae that may bloom inside the pipes and other areas that you cannot get to. It will smother the algae and once it is exposed to air and allowed to dry out for a while, it should not pose the problem of re-infecting the pool when it is refilled. Acid washing the pool will remove any left over silver that has attached itself to the surface.

Before you acid wash and drain the pool, there are a few things you need to do. You have to remove all metal items in the pool: the lights and ladders, for instance. Acid will ruin the metal objects and make your customer very unhappy. Just in case you do not know this, if you want to paint a metal object that is coated in zinc, or is galvanized, or chrome, if you treat it with muriatic acid, it chemically preps the metal so that the paint can adhere to it. (Tin roofs can be painted once you acid wash them.)

After you have removed all the water and the fixtures, you can prepare to acid wash the pool. A big mistake that some people make is that they bring their acid jugs in the pool area and set them on the deck. If there is an acid residue on the jugs or they leak, you have just damaged a deck. Always rinse each jug well and wet the area where the jugs will sit. I like to bring them into the pool with me so that I don't have to worry about damaging a surface.

A constant water supply is very important. Some choose to let the hose run all the time, but I use a spray nozzle. I leave about a foot of water in the bottom of the pool and add about two pounds of soda ash or bicarb in the pool to help neutralize the acid. I take my plastic water jug that I have drilled the holes out a little larger to, about an eighth of an inch, and mix about an ounce of tile soap with two parts water with one part acid. The soap slows the runoff down so the concentrated mixture stays on the pool surface a little longer.

Before I get ahead of myself I must tell you that different

surfaces are cleaned differently. The older plaster, referred to as Marcite can be scrubbed until you have removed the surface. As long as the acid is on the surface and is scrubbed, it continues to eat the plaster. You can actually go deeper with these surfaces than with some of the newer ones. The new exposed aggregate surfaces do not require scrubbing. You apply the acid and when the foaming stops, the job is over. You can reapply the acid solution over the area that is just cleaned and it will just run off clear. Leaving it on for too long will etch the surface. Testing a small area is essential to determine the best procedure to use. Remember you are trying to clean off build-up on a surface, not repair damage. It is best to work with someone who has done a few acid washes first before you try it on your own. Experience is the key here.

I clean all the ledges, steps, and walls first and rinse them very well. No acid product should set on them. Most steps and ledges are not perfectly level and the acid mixture can sit without running off. Once you rinse these places and they look okay, rinse them again. Better to be safe than sorry later.

On the newer surfaces, I start out with about an eight-foot section of wall. I pour the acid on the surface being careful to get an even coat on the area where I am. I watch the action of the acid on the wall and once the foaming stops or about 30 to 45 seconds have passed, I rinse the area off well. The reason I stop after 45 seconds even if the acid is still cleaning is to give the surface a break. I can always redo that area. You may find that you have to increase the ratio of acid to water. Some stubborn stains may even require a 1 to 1 ratio but be very careful before going to this strong of solution. This is where years of experience come into play. After I am satisfied with what I have done or there is no more reaction to a certain area,

I proceed to the next area. I continue this until I have gone around the entire wall surface of the pool. During this time, it may be necessary to turn on the pump that was put inside the main drain after I removed the cover and let more water out. If you have used a lot of acid, it may be necessary to add more soda ash to neutralize the acid. You do not want to have a bath of acid working on one spot in the pool or you will sure see it when you are done.

Then comes the floor time. It is best to have all the water drained at this time so that water does not stand with a concentration of acid soaking the floor surface. Start at the highest point in the pool or we call it the shallow end. Flow the acid well to cover the floor surface evenly on a section. After it has set for the proper time or you have the result you want, rinse it really well. This is the time you can probably remove the spray nozzle and just let the hose run. Continue this process until the complete floor of the pool is done.

If you notice some areas that are not clean, you can hit them again with the solution and see if you get any reaction. A wet surface does not look like a dry one. It may be hard to judge what it looks like. Make sure during the process you spray the walls and floor with clean water. Keep the surface hydrated. Once the pool is empty, I like to get a five-gallon bucket filled with water and a quarter cup of soda ash and set the pump in it. That makes sure the acid is neutralized and damage will not occur to the pump. Turn the pump on and let it circulate the clean water before you put it up.

After the job is complete, the first thing I do is install the main drain cover. Once that is done, I let the hose run. Then I start installing the fixtures back in the pool, occasionally spraying the surface down. When finished I clean up the pool area and leave the inside of the pool. Remember that I said I like to bring the jugs of acid into the pool with me? I have to take them out. It is a good idea to spray the surface of the pool deck very well with water and make sure the acid jugs are not dripping. Carefully take them away from the deck and onto an area of grass or dirt until loaded on your truck. Straight acid on a pool deck will leave a mark of some kind. Being careful is important.

Now on a pool that has cured, if the water is shut off for a while it usually is not a problem. On a surface that is still curing, up to 18 months, the flow of water must not be stopped for any period of time or a ring may develop on the surface that will never come out. This is extremely important to new or resurface surfaces on the first fill. I tell my customers that if they need to turn the water off to take a shower or to wash dishes, then do it and turn the water back on. Filling the pool back up as fast as possible is important.

Now the fire-up as we call it after re-filling has a procedure. If the water that is put into the pool has minerals or metal in it, you should be careful not to shock it until you have either removed the metals or used a metal control that has a chelating agent in it. It is important to test the source water to get an idea of what you have to deal with. If it is okay, I shock the pool hard with a non-stabilized chlorine like a liquid or calcium hypochlorite to kill the bacteria from the source water and put a chlorine residue into the water. Once the level of chlorine drops below a 5.0 ppm reading, you can test and adjust the water to the proper levels. As long as a sanitizer is introduced into the water, you do not have to hurry to adjust the other areas unless it is on a new pool surface. We will get into them later. Let the water circulate and then correct any levels of chemistry that you need to. Do not add much of any product. It is always easier to add a little more than to take away. Remember, the volume that you estimated is only an estimation or an educated guess.

After the chemicals are balanced, the job is over. It should look better than it did before you started. Do not promise customers that a certain stain or spot will come out and will be unnoticeable. It does not work that way. Tell them only what is true. It is a trial to see if you can remove the imperfections or build-up that is noticeable to them. Most likely, it will look better, but it is not a cure for everything. Acid washing is the first step and if that does not satisfy your client, you have to resurface the pool.

If you are a pool owner and not a professional, at this point you may skip ahead. Some people notice an eye-sore, and they always remember it whenever they pass by. Those people you just cannot satisfy. God knows we try. On pool surfaces, there is an industry wide problem with streaking or different shades due to the dyes in the product. There are many different causes for a surface to have streaks and most are out of our control. Some of the people who resurface pools will always blame the chemistry of the water. It usually is the source water that is used to fill the pool and not the chemistry, but it can happen. All manufacturers have a recommended level of pH and other factors for the pool during the curing process. It is highly advisable that you follow those recommendations. Everyone is a water expert and most have different ideas. Some are good and some are not. The manufacturers' recommendations should be the place to start.

PRIMING THE PUMP

When you install a new pump or have an old one torn apart and put back together, you need to prime the pump. I know the box says, "self-priming." That refers to a proper water level in the trap of the motor and once it takes in water through the impeller and through the diffuser, it creates suction and starts the water flowing.

Priming a new pump or an existing one that you have taken apart for inspection and or repair is very simple. Remove the lid on the trap and fill with water. The water level will always drain to a specified point. You can add water all day and it will just run down the suction line to the pool. Just fill it equal to the opening of the intake line and reinstall the lid. Make sure you lube the seal between the lid and the pump—or I should say first—make sure that there IS a seal between the lid and the pump body. Most are o-rings but some are square. You need to make sure that they fit properly and are lubricated. When tightening the pool trap lid, do not over tighten. Usually just snug is all you need. A good seal is one that when the pump is turned on the suction pulls the lid tighter. When you shut a pump off, the pressure is equalized and usually there is a small squirt if water comes from the lid and body. If it does not leak anymore, do not tighten it anymore. Over tightening may result in your not being able to get the lid off without damaging something.

CHECKING FOR SUCTION LEAKS

Now if you have followed the correct procedure as stated above and the pump still will not prime, here are a few tricks. Turn off all valves except the closest skimmer line; if the skimmer has the proper water level. If it will still not prime, you may have a suction leak in the line. The most common place is the fitting in front of the pump where it screws into the trap body. Instead of adding silicone and glue to see if that will correct the problem, just take a roll of electrical tape and wrap it tight around the fitting and the body of the pump. If you get a good tight wrap, it will seal most suction leaks. A good sign that the leak is in that spot is if the electrical tape actually sucks into the area between the threads on the fitting and the body.

If this is it, the repair may be simple. The simplicity of this repair can be traced to the person who installed the equipment. If a union coupling was used on the line to the front of the pump, it is simple to unscrew it, remove the fitting, and reseal. I use Teflon tape and also a silicone adhesive product. Teflon tape will harden and crack causing a poor seal after water with chemicals have passed through it and also from the vibration of the pump and the water flowing through the lines. Regular plumbers' pipe-joint cement will fail after a while also.

If the pump has run dry and has been hot to the point of turning the PVC piping brown from heat or has melted the trap basket, you need to check this fitting automatically. I have seen pumps that were so hot they expanded and the fittings could just be pulled right out of the pump. Usually after the pump cools off, they come back to shape. Do not add cold water in a hot pump. It is like a radiator on your car. You can crack the ceramic seal between the impeller and seal plate. Let it cool first and more times than not, the pump will continue to perform the way it did before getting hot. Remember, if you have a pump that has done this, there is a reason and you have to find out the reason and correct it. They don't just melt down for the fun of it.

Some of the reasons for a pump to lose its prime are that it may have a leak that siphons the water out of the pump when shut off. The most common problem, other than a bad lid seal, is that the water level is too low and the skimmers cannot supply the pump with adequate water. Something is stuck in the weir of the skimmer or stuck in the skimmer causing a disruption of water supply to the skimmer that can cause a skimmer to suck air. I have seen cleaner-hoses in front of a skimmer hole disrupting the flow of water to the skimmer. I have seen broken pipes that have been hit with a weed eater. I have seen o-rings in a suction valve that are worn and the lock nut on the handle of the valve being loose. All of these can cause a pump not to prime when it starts up. The list is endless and you have to be careful to make sure you find the cause and correct the problem. Remember, the suction pressure from a pump is like electricity. It is going to flow to the least resistance. It is easier to suck air than water, and it will take that path if an air leak is presented to the pump.

PUMP MOTOR REPLACEMENT

First, if you are not comfortable working with electricity and have no experience doing so, don't try replacing the pump or the motor. You can damage the pump, fry yourself, and possibly start a fire. Electricity is very dangerous and being around water makes it so much more dangerous. There is absolutely nothing to be ashamed of telling someone that you prefer not to do electrical repairs. Safety always comes first above making money. I have never seen an armored car in a funeral procession taking the dead man's money to his grave.

In this section, I am not training a novice to replace a motor.

Instead, what I am doing is going over the basics for the ones who do, kind of like a refresher course. Changing a motor for the first time requires hands on instruction and supervision by a professional whether it is in this business or a residential electrician.

Before replacing a pump motor, you need to determine that the motor is bad. The best way is to shut the power off to the motor at the breaker box. Remove the end cover to the motor. If you can turn on the power to the motor and it does not pop the breaker, take a meter and check the voltage coming into the motor. If it is 110 volts, you have to put the common test lead on-the-ground wire and the hot lead on the feed line. If voltage is detected on both lines, you have power running through the motor. If you do not, the problem is elsewhere. On 220-volt motors, putting the test leads on each of the lines coming into the motor should show 220 volts. If you only detect 110 volts, the problem is elsewhere.

If the proper voltage is there, more than likely the motor is bad. In Florida, motors are outside and exposed to the elements, After a motor is a few months old, it is usually not possible to have it rebuilt or have a bearing replaced. Replacing motors is usually cheaper than repairing them.

If you do not have the proper voltage, you need to check the source. The breaker that is dedicated to that pump is a good place to start. If you have voltage at the breaker, you know the problem is between the breaker and the motor. If you are not comfortable and are experienced in checking electricity, do not take that cover off of the panel of the supply box. Almost everything in there is waiting to flow electricity to something. Your standing on the ground makes a perfect ground for electricity to go through you, and you will be history. The main line coming into a main power supply does not have a GFI breaker or any kind of breaker at all. At 220 volts and 120 amps, your chance for survival does not look good.

If your problem is in between the motor and the pump, it could be in the time clock or the system control. It could be a broken wire that multiplies the danger of looking for a problem. Pumps that use a metal conduit are dangerous if a wire is broken in them, and if they touch the walls of the conduit, it is not any different than a wire except that touching it could fry you. If you know what you are doing and you change a motor, it is a good idea to change the metal conduit to a non-conductive conduit. Safety is the name of the game. Also a little advice: when you change a motor or work on electricity on a system, you are responsible if someone gets hurt or is killed. Know what you are doing and be properly trained.

Now that you have determined that the motor is bad, you need to disassemble it. First, make sure that the power source is turned off by testing for current at the motor. Do not trust your test meter either. Find a known good power source to see if your meter is working properly, and if it passes the test, then test your motor wiring. If you are sure you have no power to the motor and if it is possible to get to, take the wiring off first and remove the wires and conduit away from the motor. That keeps you from being in water when you break the pump apart. On the end of the wires that attach to the connectors of the motor, use wire nuts on the end to keep them from coming in contact with anything in case the power is turned on. If it has a blade connector attached to wire for a quick connection, wrap them in electrical tape to achieve the same safe effect.

Different pumps have different disassembly methods. Some are bolted on to the main body, and some use a quick connection ring so that when the motor is in place the ring simply holds it with an o-ring surrounding the motor housing or the seal plate. These are quick, and chances for your warping a seal plate or housing adapter are low.

Once you either unbolt the pump or remove the retaining lock ring, you should be able to pull the pump out of the front housing. Once the pump is removed from the housing and you have it in your hands, take it to a place where you can work comfortably and a place where if you drop a part or bolt it is easy to find. The grass is not a good place to work. Too many times I have had to go get small parts because I lost them in grass. I use the tailgate of my truck as a work area. Usually if something falls, it stays on the tailgate.

At the rear of the motor, there is usually a cut out piece of the shaft where a wrench can be put on the shaft to hold it while you are removing the impeller. With some models of motors, you have to remove the capacitor to get access to put a wrench on the shaft. Special tools are available for either a closed or open impeller to remove it without damage. I have used a large pair of channel locks with a cloth between the impeller and the tool to loosen the impeller when it can be unscrewed off. I would recommend that you purchase the proper tools to prevent damage and do the job right. Damage to an impeller, even small, can disrupt the flow of water and affect the efficiency of the pump. It can also cause a noticeable noise from the pump. After the impeller is removed, usually the seal plate comes right off if it is not a bolt-on kind that acts as a motor mounting bracket and seal plate combination. Either way you have to unbolt the mounting bracket from the motor.

Now after all the parts have been disassembled, clean them up. Remove the seal from the seal plate and inspect for damage. Carefully inspect the impeller for damage debris inside the veins of the impeller and be careful to look at the end that the shaft seal goes against to make sure there are no cracks and that the threads are not worn or damaged. Look at the seal plate and see if there are any cracks or areas where water has leaked and see if the leak was caused by a bad seal or a defect. Once the cleaning and inspection are done to your satisfaction, it is time to reassemble.

First, remove the end cover to the new motor. On a motor that can be operated by either 110 volts or 220 volts, make sure that it is set for the proper voltage that is servicing the motor. Not being set correctly can result in a motor that does not work or can burn a new motor up. Refer to the manufacturer's label on the motor for instruction. If the mounting bracket bolts to the motor, go ahead and install that. Make sure that it is put on correctly. Some tell you by having the top printed on them, but all will have a slot for water to drain on the bottom of the bracket. Just in case the seal leaks slightly, the water does not go into the motor assembly. Before you install the seal plate, you need to install a new seal. Do not use the same seals and gaskets that were taken off the motor. Always replace with new ones.

The ceramic shaft seal comes with a rubber o-ring or a rubber cover for the back of the seal that fits into the seal plate. If an o-ring, make sure to lube it well. If it has the other, I always put a little silicone around the cover at the bottom to aid in sealing in the seal plate. Make sure you do not get silicone on the shaft seal and it is recommended that you do not get your finger on the surface also. Body oils can sometimes create a bad seal.

Install the seal plate if it is not a bolt-on model and make sure it is in the right position. Install the shaft seal on the impeller or the shaft depending on which pump that you have. Make sure you lube the rubber seal parts but do not get any lube on the ceramic part. Carefully install the seal in the right location. Ceramic seals must touch each other. Do not install it wrong, or it will have to be done again and will cost you a seal. When you have installed the seal, screw the impeller onto the shaft. After it starts compressing the motor, the shaft will turn. Put your wrench on the end of the armature of the motor where you put it for removing the impeller. I have found out that if the shaft is secured where it will not turn, a good strong hand tightening with both hands is usually good enough. When the motor starts, it will tighten the impeller by spinning.

After the impeller has been installed, a diffuser will go over the impeller and mount to the seal plate. If it came with an impeller ring, make sure you have re-installed it or you may not get the pump to prime. At this time you can install whatever o-rings and seals that are required for the pump that you have and re-install the motor into the housing of the pump. Secure the motor either by the lock ring or by bolts. Be careful not to over-tighten the bolts that connect the motor and front housing. It is easy to warp the seal plate causing problems.

After it is assembled, install a new o-ring on the lid for the trap, add water to prime the pump, and install the lid to a snug fit. Secure the electrical connections last and turn on the power. Make sure you connect the bonding wire back to the motor and any exterior grounding before turning on the power. If everything has been done right and you have no external leaks, the pump should prime. Once the pump has primed, check for leaks at the equipment and look at the water flow. A circulation pump trap lid should be clear and free of bubbles when the pump is running properly. Any bubbles indicate a suction leak, and a partially full trap of water usually indicates a restriction in the suction line or cavitations caused by a pressure side restriction or a plugged impeller. A circulation pump that is flowing with only a limited amount of water in the trap could be a sign of a restriction on the suction side of the system. It could be a restriction in a line or simply a valve being partially turned off. If the pump has a roaring action to the water in the trap, it is a good sign that the pump is sucking water but also is sucking air from somewhere. If the water has to travel upward or from a long distance, it is probably normal and should clear up in a few minutes.

Turn the pump off and let it set a few minutes while you look for an indication of a leak. A leak in the pump housing causing the water in the pump to drain out overnight will surely cause the pump to melt down when it tries to start up for its cycle. Having this situation is not a good position to be in when looking for job advancement.

CHAPTER 11

Winterizing Your Pool or Spa

Procedures and ideas for winterizing vary from one person to another and also from one area to another. The more extreme low temperatures, the more drastic the measures you use to protect the equipment and pool. Here in Central Florida it does freeze at times but normally the freezing temperatures occur in early morning and do not last long enough to do damage to exposed pipes and equipment. Pool owners reap this benefit but the professional is denied a very profitable procedure that the other areas have to perform.

If you are in an area where the water table is low so that there is a low chance of a pool popping out of the ground, it may be best to drain all the water. I personally do not like this idea because it is my belief that if you remove the water you release a lot of pressure that is holding the pool in place. If the compaction of the soil underneath the pool is not kept at a constant pressure, soil can shift because of rain and snow runoff around the pool shell. As you re-fill the pool, movement can happen. I have seen filled pools that have moved and pulled away from the deck and sunk somewhat because of clay soils or improper compaction of soils. Some are the result of the builder's not doing something right pertaining to the different types of soil, and some are just the area you live in. In Florida, we have sinkhole problems. We are sitting on voids in the ground that can cause the earth to sink and the ground above goes into a hole. Most are small but I have seen some that have caused enough damage to have a home condemned.

Take a plastic 16-ounce water bottle and fill it to the top. You secure the lid back on and place it in your freezer. The next day you inspect this bottle and find it is cracked, the lid has popped off, or it has swollen all out of shape. This is due to expansion when a liquid freezes. Expansion is the reason water pipes burst in the winter. Realizing this, you can apply that theory to the procedure you will use on the pools in your particular area.

Anything that has water in it and is exposed above ground can freeze causing damage.

Equipment that is located underground in a room by the pool also needs to be protected and drained to protect it unless the pool is heated for the winter. A leak in an underground pump room can result in extensive damage and expensive repairs.

In colder areas, wrapping pipes with insulation and covering them with a plastic wrap may help protect the pipes but when water is not flowing through these pipes the lines need to be drained. The object is to have no broken pipes or frozen equipment.

The first thing to winterizing the pool is to make sure the pool is free of algae and that all minerals in the water are removed and a chelating agent is put into the pool to keep the minerals from coming out of solution and attaching to the surface. Algae normally will not form when the temperature of water drops below 55ºF. To make sure it is dead, shock the pool by raising the chlorine residue to 30 to 50 ppm of chlorine and let the pump run overnight. Once the chlorine level has returned to a level of 5.0 ppm or lower, you can adjust the rest of your chemicals.

If you used a metal remover that has phosphates in it, you might need to remove the phosphates before shutting the pool down since they will feed the algae if it forms. What metal is left in the pool water the chelating agent will help keep them in suspension. As you can see, winterizing a pool is not going to be a one-day affair.

When all this has been done, you can start to remove the water. I like to take the water level down well below the return fittings and below the light to prevent ice that may form from cracking the light assembly when expansion occurs. It also protects the niche that the light sits in. Some are plastic type niches and could be damaged if ice puts pressure on them. The pool water level will be lowered by two to three feet depending on the placement of the returns and light. This amount of water will also remove some TDS in the water as well as calcium and stabilizer levels that may need to be lowered. If you used the pool circulation pump to lower the water by turning off the skimmers and only pull water through the main drain, turn off the valve that is releasing the water and let it circulate back into the pool. At this time I like to shock it again. I prefer to use dichlor. It dissolves fast and is stabilized. Mix it in a bucket of water and with the pool running pour the solution around the pool and let it circulate. If the pump is circulating with no stress or signs that it may lose a prime, leave it on for a while to distribute the chlorine and get it into solution.

Now that you have drained the water, added chlorine, and

adjusted the balance of the water, it is time to shut it down. First, turn off all the power supplies to all equipment. That means any timers, lights, and everything that is connected to the swimming pool. I used to take either wide masking tape or duct tape and cover the breakers and write on them with a magic marker to leave off. The next step is to drain the equipment. Most pool products have drain plugs for removing the water in them. I prefer to remove the circulation pump(s), clean them thoroughly, and store them inside in a dry place. When I do this, I make sure that I take an air compressor and blow the water out of the pump and blow air into the back of the motor to remove any debris that has settled inside the motor assembly. I take duct tape and seal the back of the motor so that ants and bugs cannot get into the motor and make a nest. I leave the lid for the trap off, and I will tell you why in a few minutes.

Next step is to break the filter down. I hope that before you started this procedure you backwashed the filters very well. On a sand filter remove the lower drain plug and drain all the water out. Leave the plug out and put it in the trap basket of the pump. All drain plugs should go into the trap basket so that you know where they are. Turn the valve to backwash so that air can come into the filter and prevent an airlock so that all the water has a chance to escape. Once the water has drained out, you can use either a shop vacuum or an air compressor to help force all the water out or vacuum it out. Remember if you are using the air method, limit your pressure to about 30 psi so that you do not damage anything. You can shoot air into the waste port to remove the water that is trapped in the little pockets of the multi-port valve. You should put the valve in all the different positions to make sure all the water is removed from the valve. Upon completion of this task, put the filter back on the filter position to close the system to the elements. I leave the drain plug out of the sand filter tank for the winter.

On a cartridge filter, just drain it and clean the tank. Remove the filter element and clean it very well and store it inside also. Cold air and ice can damage the pleats in the element. Once all the water has been forced out of all pipes and equipment, you can re-install the lid and the drain plug. Make sure you lubricate all o-rings and seals before you totally close up everything. When you install the lid back on just snug it gently so that damage is not done to the seal when it gets cold.

On a DE filter, you can do many things. You can totally clean, drain, and dismantle the filter and remove the grids or fingers and store them, or you can just simply drain and clean the filter completely. Soak the grids or fingers if needed and re-install the grids or fingers back into the filter. If a grid or element requires cleaning with acid, it is advised that you wait until opening the pool. Acid residue will damage these things over a period of time just sitting. On filters that use a multi-port or a slide valve, you can simply unscrew the union nut holding the valve in place on the filter and move the complete filter into a dry area for protection. This way once the filter is cleaned and completely dry, it will be ready for startup the next season. Cover the inlet holes and install the drain plug so that nothing can get into the filter. If the filter was installed using unions, the valve should also be stored.

Now remove all the return nozzles off the return lines in the pool. If the trap basket is large enough to store them in, also put them in there so you have them next year. The reason for doing this is so that no water can sit and freeze, causing cracks. Take a plug that has a fitting that you can shoot air in and blow out all the lines. Sucking the lines at the return lines with a shop vacuum will also help in removing water. All lines should be blown out or vacuumed to ensure that there is no sitting water left in the line that can expand and crack a pipe. When the water level is lowered in the pool, the level of water in the pipes from the skimmer (s) and drain(s) will equal the height of the water in the pool. It is recommended that this level be a good three feet below the surface of the deck to prevent freezing. I like to use recreational vehicle anti-freeze for the skimmer and drain lines. The ideal situation is to blow all the water from the skimmer lines by using a shop vacuum. We know that all the water will not be removed, so that is why I use the RV anti-freeze. Install tapered plugs in the skimmer(s) and the lines from the pump that goes to the skimmer(s) to create a dead air space for good insulation. If you blow air down the main drain line and see air entering the pool, shut the valve off to the drain and try to create an airlock. Sometimes this works and sometimes it does not, but it's about the best you can do. Once all the lines are blown out, plug all of the lines on both sides to create a good dead air space.

If the pool is equipped with a heater, make sure that the heat exchanger has been blown out very well and that water has been removed. Turn off the gas to the heater. Some people remove the heat exchanger and store it separately. I do not do so, but I do not live in Michigan either. A good rule of thumb is to check with other professionals in your area and find out what they do. Everyone has different ways of doing things, and some may be better for your circumstance than what I have described to you. My experience working on pools in the winter is limited to southern Colorado. Winters there are not as extreme as in some areas of the country.

Now let us take a look at the water that is left in the pool. In areas that freeze regularly the water on the surface will freeze as well, especially since it is not moving. The thicker the ice may become, the greater the pressure that is being forced onto the walls of the pool. I have heard the pressure can actually crack a pool wall. Therefore, what you have to do is make a pressure relief. It is a very simple procedure. You take gallon milk and water jugs that have been cleaned and put a small amount of water in them just enough so they sink a few inches but still float. Drop them into the pool. Gravel actually works best but if a jug get ruptured, you have gravel all in the drain lines, which will restrict the flow and can permanently clog up the lines when other debris gets into the lines. When the water freezes and starts to expand, the ice has a place to go. It will force pressure to the jugs and they collapse to a certain degree to relieve pressure off the walls. Also drop one in the skimmer. Since the holes are plugged if any water gets trapped into the skimmer, it also has its relief.

Now that everything is drained and plugged so nothing can get into them, you have to make a decision on what to do about this hole in the ground that is partially empty. This is the time that I consider the pool at its most dangerous. It is easy to fall into a pool and there is not enough water in it that it can prevent injury. Also if a small child or elderly person falls into the pool, the freezing temperatures of the water causes them to go into hypothermia and could very easily result in death. Proper fencing off and covering is recommended. If you only throw a tarp over the pool and it rains or snows, the weight will force the cover onto the surface of the water, letting it trap debris which will be difficult to get out of the pool. What is needed is either some type of pillow or PVC frame that will actually hold the cover up and preferably make like a tent so that debris and moisture can flow off the cover and away from the pool. It must be secured tightly by the use of water tubes or sand bags with tie-downs. Water tubes will also freeze so keep that in mind when using them. Do not fill them all the way to insure they can expand. Not only do you not want to get debris and critters in the pool but you want it sealed well enough so that wind cannot get underneath the cover and rip it off. The better the pool is sealed and protected, the easier it will be to start it up when season starts.

For a spa that is part of the pool or above the pool with a waterfall effect, it is better just to drain all of it and blow out and plug all lines including the main drain. Add a little RV antifreeze to the main drain line and in the drain itself to prevent freezing. It would help if you put a smaller plastic bottle with water in it so the water that might get trapped in the drain has a place to expand. Cover it properly to keep debris out and to keep people and critters from getting hurt or killed.

If a portable spa is being shut down for the winter, you perform the same tasks of draining and blowing out lines. Spas have piping that runs horizontal all around the spa. Some water will get trapped. The pump or pumps are usually the lowest part of a system other than some plumbing and it is a good idea to remove them and store them also. Once you are convinced that all the water that you can get out is gone, seal it up also. Cover it and you are done.

One of the reasons we drain water out of pools is for the tiles that are at the top of the shell at the water line. They will crack easier than the shell will if freezing occurs. There are many different ideas and beliefs about winterizing a pool. Some feel that you can just lower the water a little and leave the pump running constantly like an outside water faucet and it will do a job. That may work, depending on the temperature, but if anything ever happens like a power outage and the circulation stops, it is the wrong time to try to winterize the system. Prevention is the key here.

Liner pools are a different monster. On an on-the-ground pool you can simply perform the same procedures with the equipment and simply drain the pool down below the skimmer line. Do this after you have balanced the water and shocked the pool. Lithium hypochlorite is ideal for liner pools. Remove the line going into the bottom of the skimmer and leave it open. This does two things. If additional water enters the pool, it will drain out and you do not have to seal the skimmer with plugs. Use a larger pillow to hold the cover up high and also put in several jugs with a little water in them to help with the expansion. Heavy freezing on an on-the-ground pool could cause the walls to split from expansion. You need to secure the pillow or pillows so that they stay in the center and movement is limited. Secure the cover really well so it does not blow off. Freezing temperatures are not good for a liner. It might do so much damage that the liner may crack and damage the pool. You will have to determine what to do based on the area you live in or ask a professional for the best procedure to use. With expansion of the pool walls, you should be okay depending on the extent of the temperatures and the length of freezing. Leaving a pump running in the winter on an on-the-ground pool is not recommended since they typically have a problem with circulation to begin with.

An in-ground pool liner is a totally different breed of animal.

You face the weakness of the walls and the damage that can be done by the freezing temperatures on the liner itself. There are not many in-ground liner pools way up north. Since most of the in-ground liner pools that I dealt with in the cold country were indoor pools, I have not been required to protect one.

Large rectangular pool

The procedure that I have been told by some different service companies is that you perform the same tasks on the chemistry and the equipment as you do on the concrete pools. You only drain the water level down about eight inches. The reason for the eight inches is for rain or snow runoff that might go in to the pool. If it is covered, lower the water to the bottom of the skimmer. Plug the return lines and get all the water out that you can. One way to get all or most of the water out of a line that is lower than the water level is to have plugs that have small valves installed in them and simply install the plug, add a piece of small hose onto the valve, vacuum that out with a shop vacuum, and while the vacuum is still running shut the valve off, and you have a dry line. You can also drain the pool down below the returns. Plug the lines after they have drained and refill the pool to the level that you desire. These plugs you naturally leave in. Seal the other end of the return lines. If you really are concerned about the temperatures, you could dive down and perform the same procedure on the main drain line and then add a little RV antifreeze into it for security. If the level of water is too low, the liner could rip when you fill it up. Make sure that the beaded liner is in the channel properly and is secured by a product we refer to as liner lock. It is cheap and necessary for a secure fit of the bead inside the channel. This should have been used when the liner was initially installed but sometimes it is not. If you live in a very cold climate and have an in-ground liner pool that is exposed to the elements, please check with local professionals for their advice on winterizing your pool. They have gone through trials and errors and know what works and what does not for that area. Do not get only one opinion but try for several just to be on the safe side.

RESTARTING THE POOL

When you winterized the pool, you documented each pool and what type, size, and brand of equipment that is installed on every pool. The reason for doing so is that when you go around and start to fire them back up you will have extra o-rings and seals for that brand and type of equipment so you do not have to drive back and forth to the supply house.

First order of business is to remove the cover. If the cover has settled and has water on the top, you need to take a pump like a cover pump that uses a water hose that drains the water off and out of the hose. After the cover is drained and as much of the debris has been removed, it is time to take it off the pool, being careful not to drop too much junk on the surface of the water. Make sure you clean and protect it to the manufacturer's recommendation before storing it. It needs to be dry most of all.

Now that you have taken the cover off, you get your first look at the pool. If you did a good job, the water should be fairly clean. If you have a lot of debris in the pool, you might want to use a portable pump system to vacuum the debris to waste before adding water and contaminating it. Remove all of the plugs and areas that were duct taped. You may have to use a cleaner such as acetone to remove the adhesive that came off from the tape or another suitable cleaner. Acetone does an excellent job but static electricity is enough to ignite it. Always use in open air and be careful. You can install the return nozzles and your equipment. Open it all up and inspect for foreign objects and critters that may have gotten in them. Clean and unseal all of it and using new o-rings and seals, replace the equipment back to the way it was and you are almost there.

After all the equipment is back in place and all plugs have been put back in and lubed, make sure the pumps have water in them for start up. Bring the water up to proper levels and you are ready to go. Turn the power back on to the equipment and turn the pump on. Once it primes, check for leaks and look at the water returning back to the pool. If rust or other deposits have formed, they will come out in force. This is the time that you can adjust your nozzles to get the flow and circulation that you want for that pool.

After everything is done and running with no leaks, it is time to take care of the water. Bring the balance in order and have the pH be no more than 7.4. Remember the lower the pH, the better the sanitizer works. After the chemistry is right, you need to shock the pool to kill the bacteria and whatever critters have gotten into the water. If signs of algae are present, you want to treat that also. Let the pool run for 48 hours. Not only does this make sure everything has circulated into the solution, it also puts pressure on the equipment and lets it get warm to see if you are going to have any premature failures. This is the time to make sure all sanitizing equipment is functioning properly and delivering the proper amount of sanitizer.

After the balance is good and the water has been shocked and cleaned, you just wait for the temperature to come up and enjoy the season.

If you have a heater for the pool that operates on gas or propane, it is a good idea to have a service man come and check the heater before startup. Most pool professionals cannot work on the gas part of a heater unless they are certified to do so. It is good to have a professional perform the initial fire-up of the heater to check for proper operation and make sure it is functioning properly. We used to have one follow us or have a day that he can just go by each heated pool and perform his safety check. Better to be safe.

MILD WINTERS

If you live in a place like Florida where the freezes do no damage because they are short, you normally run your pump a few hours a day. When it comes time to open your pool for swimming, it is a good time to clean your filter before the season kicks off. Sand filters should be able to go three years without changing the sand if used in normal conditions. A DE filter should be cleaned every year. Checking levels of calcium and stabilizer as well as TDS is recommended so that if water needs to be replaced, it is done at the start of the season. Water takes a while to warm up and draining your pool in the middle of the season may require some time to warm back up.

Starting a new swimming season that goes without problems ensures that you will have this client for the next season. If proper levels of chemistry have been corrected, the less time you will have to spend on this pool during the season. It always seems that when something happens to a pool is when the owner has something planned for that time. Early prevention saves a lot of work and the satisfaction of having happy customers makes you feel like you have a purpose. Occasionally they may brag on their pool man, but I guarantee this. If the owner has had problems or is dissatisfied, everyone will know.

***Freeform pool* 2**

When you have a pool for a time you will know if it is a pool that has problems. The start of the season is the time to find out what you can do to solve the problems that you have had with a particular pool. Perform good tests. A pool that has given you problems the previous season and when testing the water you cannot come up with a solution, a good place to start is to change some water.

Now I do not like to waste water. My water was in my pool for 16 years. Some believe that water just gets old. There may be something to this theory. When I have decided to drain water out of a pool to help with a problem when I cannot determine the cause, it seems to help. A TDS meter will be one of the best tools that you can use. You can determine that strange problems that do not seem to respond to your treatments usually have to do with high levels of TDS. Unfortunately, the tests do not tell you what levels are high and what to look for. If you continue to have a problem with a particular pool and you really want to keep this customer, it may be wise to have an independent company that deals in detailed water testing perform a test to determine what is in the water that would cause the problem. I have not run into this problem but I have heard of those who have. My last resort is to replace some water with fresh and it seems to fix the problem. Better yet, have two samples tested. One is the pool water and the other is the source water. If the source water is contaminated with something, putting the same water back in will not help.

CHAPTER 12

Pool Heating

There are three basic types of heaters for the pool, electrical, which is very expensive, solar, and combustion-type heaters. A combustion-type of heater is one that uses fuels that burn to create the heat source for heating the water. They come in fuel oil, propane, natural gas, and wood heaters.

Now electric heaters are rare because of the expense of electricity to heat a pool. The prices of electricity have risen so that it is not very economical. Electric heaters work well with spas and hot tubs, and they are able to maintain a certain temperature.

Heat pumps for pools simply pull the heat from the atmosphere and transfer it to the water in your pool. The same function is used on your home heat pump. The best heat pumps have titanium piping that resists the chemicals that we use. The newer heat pumps are more efficient than earlier ones were, and running a heat pump to keep a steady temperature of the water in a pool is much cheaper. If you want to heat your pool only a couple of times a year, gas may be cheaper, and it will take less time to bring up temperature than a heat pump.

The best models reverse themselves and can cool a pool using the same procedure. It takes the temperature from the water and transfers it to the air. In the heat position, the water flows from the pool and into the heater. It forces the water through a heat exchanger, which is heated by Freon flowing through the coiled tubing that makes up the piping in the heat exchanger. The temperature from the Freon is transferred to the water and is a lower temperature than it was upon entering the heat exchanger. The Freon flows back to the evaporator where it picks up heat from the atmosphere and reheats the Freon. The longer the heater runs, the hotter the water gets. It does have lower and higher limits.

On larger pools multiple heat pumps can be used. There are also heat pumps that have a defrost mode for the upper northern states.

Solar heating is a great way to heat a pool. Different areas may not let a solar pool system work well, but installers in your area can advise you. Always get a couple of estimates, and if you can talk with people who have solar heating, find out the best installers and technicians that work on solar systems. Warranty is also a thing to research. Remember a company that offers the best warranty usually has a good system. Look for the length of time the company has been in service and check the with the local Better Business Bureau. Many people have gotten ripped off by inferior systems that do not perform correctly. The customer always loses. They may win a court battle but they still lose. When things like that happen, their pool has lost its charm.

Let us say that we have a good solar system installed on our pool. Did I forget to tell you the best part of a solar system? After the system is installed and paid for, that is the end of the expense of the system. It operates when the pool pump does.

Back to the subject at hand. Solar heated pools pump water that leaves the filter and flows through a collector, which I call panels. These panels absorb the heat from the sun, and it transfers to the water and is returned back to the pool. It is the same idea with the heat pump. Most good systems have a sensor installed to detect the temperature of the water. If it rises above the set temperature, the water flow is shut off. Once the temperature is dropped, the valve opens again to allow water to enter the panels. It can also work in reverse. If the panels have no sun on them, they can actually cool a pool down. If you want to cool a pool down, you can run the pool at night. Where we are located, you can use a pool up to 10 to 11 months depending on our weather pattern. Pretty neat, right? There's more. You have all heard about solar covers. If you were told that by putting this cover on a pool it would raise the temperature many degrees and you believed it, I have some land in the Everglades I want to sell you. It does not happen. A solar cover is designed to help keep the temperature of the water in your pool and reduce evaporation. It does work and is needed for solar as well as the other systems to trap the heat in the pool. It saves a lot of money to use a solar cover. Unfortunately, a pool that is irregularly shaped is hard to cover with a solar cover.

Evaporation is described as a form of vaporization. That is the process whereby atoms or molecules in a liquid gain enough energy to enter a gaseous state, the opposite of condensation. When this occurs, the water in the gas state rises because it weighs less than the water. The colder temperatures of the atmosphere attract the higher temperatures of the water causing the gas to rise. This is the reason that more people think they have leaks when the temperature drops at night in the summer months.

Fuel oil heaters are still used in the states where they have to use heating oil to heat their homes. I personally have not worked on a fuel oil heater on a pool but have seen a few here on older homes that use fuel oil as a source of heat. The efficiency of the heater depends on the unit itself. Sometimes the cost of fuel oil can exceed the price of propane. A report that I read stated that a 20′ by 40′ pool in Rhode Island with the temperature kept at 83oF with the prices of fuel oil at two dollars a gallon would cost up to $3,700 to heat for five months. At the same temperature and if propane was only a $1.50 for a gallon it would cost up to $3,500 to achieve the same results. With these figures, you can compare the price differences.

Wood heat requires physical work and lot of dead trees. Unless pellets are used to feed the heater automatically, someone has to fuel the fire with wood. If you have an endless supply of wood, it may be cheap to use. No electricity is involved since most wood heaters just heat water and not control the temperature. Specs on some of the heaters are that they can heat a 16′ x 32′ pool with a volume of 20,000 gallons in 48 hours from a temperature of 60oF to 85oF. They advertise that the water coming out of the heater is three to five degrees warmer than when it entered the heater. That is determined by the type of wood you use and what the British Thermal Unit (BTU) of the wood you are using is. That is not bad. Wood heaters can produce up to 100,000 BTUs plus.

The advantage to this type of heating is that it takes less time to heat the water a few degrees. So if the temperature drops five degrees, it will not take as long to bring it back up to where you want it. To save money, a little labor may be worthwhile.

Gas and propane heaters are very common. They are efficient

and are getting better all the time. They also can perform many functions. Some can be programmed so the pool and spa mode have different heat settings. They come with safety features that limit the temperature and also will not open the gas valve until proper flow of water is reached. This keeps the heater from melting the heat exchanger by heating it without proper cooling. The flow of water prevents the temperature from becoming dangerous to the unit itself.

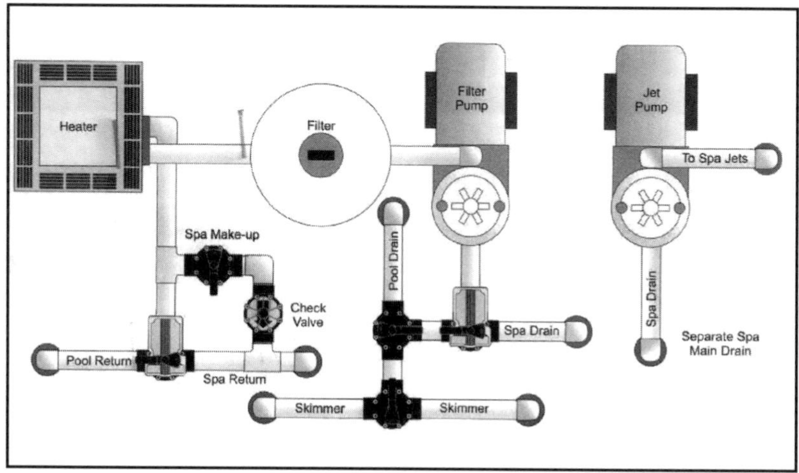

Basic pool and spa combination using separate pumps to circulate the pool and spa with a heater installed

When sizing a pool heater, make sure you know what you are doing. Ask the manufacturer or refer to their specification sheets for the proper heater for your pool's size. Also specify whether it is gas or propane. The pressures are different on these products, and different size orifices must be used on propane than on gas. The altitude also depends on which size orifice is used on both models.

The orifice is a restrictor that will let only a certain amount of gas pass through it at a precise pressure. If they are not sized right, your efficiency can be altered, resulting in higher fuel costs. Gas professionals should be the only ones installing gas in a heater. You can install the water part, but a service person certified in gas installation and repair should be the only one working on the gas part of the heater. Unless you know your electricity, a certified electrician should be the one to hook up the electrical feed to the heater. Doing this wrong can damage the heater also.

Those above items that I have just mentioned do affect the cost of a gas or propane heater and can be quite high. When selecting a heater, you will need to take all that into consideration. In addition, if the heater is in a building or room, it has to be vented to the outside so that carbon monoxide does not fill this area. It will kill you fast with no warning. Each heater has a vent system designed for it and should not be altered. Only the approved venting system should be used.

Now recently I have had two different service calls on propane heaters. One was a unit that was tied to two propane tanks that could be controlled independently. One tank ran out of propane and the owner switched it to the other tank. When the first tank ran dry, the line had filled with air. When the other tank was turned on, the line developed an airlock trapping air between the heater and the tank. There is a very simple cure if you have a gas license. You just have to loosen the gas line coming to the heater and bleed the air out of the line. When you smell propane, you tighten the line and test it for leaks. If the leak test checks out, let the heater sit for awhile so that the propane has a chance to disperse. Propane is heavier than air. It will settle on the bottom of the heater and just sit there.

After you wait for a while, you can turn the power back on, turn the heater on, and step back. If you do not have a license for gas, leave it alone. The liability is too great if anything ever happens. I know that we all try to save our customers money and do the best job that we can for them, but it was not my fault that tank ran dry. (That is why they come with a gauge.) I have to admit that it would sure make them happy if you could fix it in a few minutes. It never fails that when you try to go beyond your scope to help someone, it always backfires on you. If you want to service heaters, go to the proper schools for the basic knowledge and get the proper license and insurance.

The second heater suffered from a rare problem that I have seen only once before. Again, this heater was a propane unit. It had a problem with the limit system that controls the water temperature. The service call was an intermittent problem. I found out that the heat had increased so much that the internal components of the heater were glowing red. The heat exchanger looked like melted metal. It got so hot that it starved itself from oxygen. It would shut down for lack of oxygen for a few minutes and then try to relight itself. The heater would try to ignite and without the proper amount of oxygen and with the extreme heat, the propane would try to burn and roared inside the heater that sound like a jet engine and the black smoke poured out of the top of the heater. When I manually shut the heater off in the control box, the heater was shut off but still supplied fuel. I had to reach around and turn the gas off. The pipes were very warm five feet from the heat sink of the heater, almost to the melting point. If I had taken off the side of the heater to inspect it, the additional oxygen would have let the gas ignite and probably would have blown up.

The reason I throw these little things into this area is that if you do not know what is happening, you have a hard time correcting it. Never be ashamed to admit that you do not know everything. All you have to know is how to be safe. As you learn in this book, a very large portion of what we handle on a daily basis is either poison or very deadly if abused. Do not go beyond your abilities or knowledge. Money is not worth it.

CHAPTER 13

Sanitizing Systems

The different types of sanitizing systems are too numerous to mention. Every company in the pool business manufactures some type of chemical feeder. It can be a simple erosion type, floating feeder to the most elaborate injection systems. We covered the salt generating systems in the previous chapter so I will not go into them.

The most basic of sanitizer feeders is the floating tablet feeder, a type of erosion feeder. It works just like its name. Either stabilized or non-stabilized tablets are put in the floater. Depending on the tablet, it can produce chlorine on a level of one to two tablets for every 10,000 gallons of water and should last about a week. It all depends on the bonding agent that a tablet was formulated with. Usually the cheaper the tablet, the quicker it dissolves.

Your goal is a safe level of sanitizer to last a certain time and not overdose the pool. Most come with slots that can be adjusted to get the proper amount of chlorine into the water. The negative factor is that they continue to chlorinate even after the pump is turned off. The process of erosion is what dissolves the chlorine and as long as the feeder is sitting in water, the product will dissolve. The product may be introduced into the pool when the pump is not running but the sanitizer will be evenly dispersed throughout the pool until the pump comes on. This is not good if the feeder is up against the wall of a liner pool or is sitting in front of the skimmer. A liner pool can be bleached by the feeder and when the pump starts up it pulls a concentrated solution of chlorine into it that can start dissolving metals. Most tablets have a low pH, and when the water is pulled into a system that is heavily chlorinated, the pH of that solution will be low and corrosive. Remember low pH and the introduction of chlorine or bromine is extremely corrosive. Bromine is far more aggressive than stabilized chlorine.

Next is the "chemical feeder." This may be an inline version that actually is installed in the line going back to the pool or an off-line version that sits away from the plumbing but has small plastic lines that run from the return line to the feeder and back to the return line for dispersion of the product. These also work by erosion and most can be adjusted to provide an even distribution of sanitizer to the pool or spa. The problem with an off-line feeder is the plastic lines can be broken easily and can degrade after a while.

Most chlorine feeders can be used with bromine. No granular products should be put in the feeder—only tablets. They can also be used with a non-stabilized chlorine tablet but once a tablet has been used in the feeder, no other type of sanitizer tablet can be used. Here is the information I mentioned previously about losing your face on a chlorine feeder. If you use trichlor tablets that is all that should ever be put into the feeder. Putting another type of tablet into this feeder can result in a chemical explosion. This is no joke. Mixing chemicals should be dealt with seriously. Chemicals cannot be mixed.

Most feeders are adjustable and only handle a certain volume of water. It all depends on plumbing, temperature, and flow. So let us say that the feeder will handle a certain volume of water. For simple calculations let's say it will do 30,000 gallons of water. You have a 15,000 gallon pool. Put tablets in the feeder, install the lid, and adjust the valve to about half the maximum that the valve can go up to. It is an erosion feeder so if you have ten tablets in the feeder, it will distribute a higher level of chlorine than a feeder with only two. Always put the same amount of tablets in the feeder at a time. After a few days, you can retest the water and see where the chlorine level is. If it is high, you can adjust the control to produce less and if it is low, you can increase the level of distribution. Most importantly, the pump must run the same amount of time every day. If you run your pump for five hours and then increase it to ten hours, the chlorine that is distributed into the pool will be twice the amount. Usually, in the winter when you turn down the time your pump runs, the chlorine level will go down also and should decrease at a stable rate. I am trying to inform you about a chemical feeder which is not only controlled by the amount of tablets that are in the body of the feeder, but also by the time that the pump runs. The valve adjustment is the third way to adjust chlorine production. It is a trial and error thing that could take you a few weeks to get down to a perfect level.

Now the problem with tablets is that the majority of them are stabilized. Let's say that the weight of a tablet is eight ounces. That is four ounces of chlorine and four ounces of stabilizer. With every tablet that is dissolved in a pool, you have just added four ounces of stabilizer. Proper control has to be used here or you will be draining the pool for too much stabilizer. Cyanuric acid was discussed in the chemical chapter.

Some pools have a liquid chlorine injector system. This is usually found in commercial pools but can be used on a residential pool. It simply injects liquid chlorine into the return line of the pool using a predetermined amount of chlorine to keep a proper level of chlorine residue in the water. Liquid chlorine is cheap but it does have its problems. It will bleach most things that it comes in contact with. In case of spills, a hazardous material spill can cost very much to clean up. Most counties and cities will do a hazardous material response and cleanup for as little as two gallons of chlorine. That can cost several thousand dollars. Also with the increasing cost of transporting the chemical due to insurance, I believe the sodium hypochlorite days are limited.

Chlorine generators were discussed in Chapter 8 under Advanced Features. They are a very economical way to sanitize a pool after the initial cost has been paid. The reason I bring this up again is for other sanitizing uses of a chlorine generator.

Chlorine generators are being installed on bromine pools. As previously discussed, sodium bromide must have a catalyst to activate it. By using a chlorine generator on a bromine pool, you can add one pound of sodium bromide to every 50-pound bag of salt. With the addition of chlorine that is steadily being produced by the generator, the bromine bank is always active.

Now the question is why have a costly chlorine generator when having a bromine pool? Bromine pools are not stabilized and the chlorine produced by the generator is also unstabilized. The advantage of this is that the chlorine residue left in the pool when the pump shuts off, there is enough chlorine residue left in the pool to keep the bromine active longer during the off cycle of filtration. The other big advantage is that most of the chlorine generators have a super-chlorination system built-in for breaking up chloramines and bromamines. With a flip of a switch or a simple program, you can shock your pool with no added chemicals. Properly used, ozone with chlorine will break up chloramines without shocking. With the chlorine generator set low, the amount of salt used will be very little and also the amount of sodium bromide will also be reduced. It is far cheaper than the cost of bromine tablets.

We can go one more step. For those who prefer ozone, you can add an ozone generator to this system also. You can limit the amount of bromine and chlorine production and have the ozone do most of the sanitation. Actually, a good Corona Discharge system for a pool runs 24 hours. It can supply ozone constantly since the life of ozone is under an hour.

OZONE

Ozone was discovered by the scientist Christian Friedrich Schonbein. in 1839 when he noticed a unique odor during electrolysis and electrical sparking experiments. He recognized the odor as the one that occurred after a lightning flash. He named the substance "ozone" after the Greek word "ozein" which means "to smell."

Ozone is "active oxygen," that contains three oxygen atoms per molecule. You can usually smell it after a rainfall. It occurs naturally in the Earth's upper atmosphere from the sun's UV rays, and in the lower atmosphere during a lightning storm. The ozone layer protects us and is the center of controversy because it is being destroyed.

A few pool professionals and probably other folks feel that ozone equipment is a scam and does not work since they cannot see it and readily test for it. That is far from the truth. In 1906, the city of Nice, France, built the first water purification plant to use ozone. It has been used since the turn of the century to purify water and waste water in municipal systems.

Los Angeles, CA., has one of the largest municipal ozone water treatment plants in the world. It has been used for more than 60 years to purify pool and spa water. In the 1940s ozone was used to purify the indoor pool water at the U.S. Naval Academy in Annapolis. It has been used since 1984 in all Olympic Games competition pools. In 1982 it became very popular to purify bottled water.

A major advantage of ozone is that it is very safe when used properly. It has no damaging effects on equipment. It leaves no chemical taste or smell and does not burn eyes or leave them red and irritated. It will not irritate or dry out skin, nose, or ears. It has no discoloring effects on clothing or hair. Most importantly, it is a strong oxidizer.

Ozone kills bacteria many times faster than chlorine or bromine. It contains no by-products. It kills all known bacteria, viruses, Giardia lamblia cysts, yeasts, molds, and mildew. It will also oxidize hydrogen sulfides, iron, manganese, arsenic, and most chlorinate hydrocarbons found in water. It dissolves in water 13 times faster than oxygen.

The technology of Ozone has developed greatly over the past few years. The United States is actually behind other countries in this technology. A company called Del Ozone in California, has more than one million ozone systems installed worldwide and is going strong. It is a strong consideration for the individual who is considering building a new pool and one that a pool professional should recommend to customers who are having irritation problems with normal sanitizers. The majority of spa manufacturers build their spas with ozone systems installed or readily plumbed to add an ozone unit.

CHAPTER 14

Pool Safety

OVERVIEW

Water safety is not only for the individual pool owner; it is a community problem. People do drown, and not all these deaths are in the family pool. Total awareness must be used at all times when there are humans swimming in any kind of water. It only takes one time to be unsafe or unprepared for a tragedy to occur.

In the United States currently, 350 children under the age of five drown in swimming pools every year. That is about 350 too many. The estimate for children treated at hospitals for submersion incidents is over 2,600. It is the number one killer of children under five years old. Parents have to be aware that even if children can swim, they are still not drown-proof. Adults should never take their eye off children when around water.

The U.S. Consumer Product Safety Commission has many publications that can be mailed or downloaded regarding water safety. For a parent or someone considering installing a pool or spa, take a look at these publications and prepare yourself.

This is just as important a chapter as the chemical and safety information that is in this book. The water can kill you or yours as fast as chemicals can if used unsafely. I believe that we are in the Fun business. In order to have Fun, there have to be rules. I have broken the rules down into sections.

POOL OWNER

1. Make sure that at least one person in the household knows Cardiopulmonary Resuscitation (CPR).

2. If the wall of the home acts as a border for one side of the pool, make sure that safety locks and alarms are installed to warn you when a door opens.

3. Have a safety fence or an approved barrier around the pool to limit access. The fence or barrier should be a minimum of 4′ in height.

4. If you own an on-the-ground pool, make sure that the ladders or steps are the type that can be removed to prevent children from getting into the pool.

5. Never let anyone use your pool or spa if it has a drain cover missing or a cleaning port for a suction cleaner left open.

6. Children with long hair should only swim wearing a swimmers′ cap or have their hair put up in a way that it cannot get sucked into a suction fitting or drain.

7. If you are building a new pool, have a Safety Vacuum Release System (SVRS) installed. It shuts

the pool pump off if it detects a blockage or loss of water flow.

8. The safest way to avoid any suction injuries or deaths is to shut the pump off when the children swim.

9. Always know how to operate your equipment in case of an emergency. Know how to shut the equipment off if needed in a hurry.

10. Keep safety devices around the pool at all times that conform to U.S. Coast Guard specifications.

11. Keep all debris and toys away form the pool deck to keep people from tripping and falling in the pool.

12. Remove automatic cleaners from the pool when children swim to prevent them from becoming entangled in the hose.

13. Do not consume alcohol when swimming.

POOL PROFESSIONAL

1. Always leave a note or let the pool owner know the condition of their pool and what if any chemicals you added. Let them know when it is safe to enter the pool.

2. Never leave any kind of chemical where the children can get to them. Also, keep them away from animals.

3. Always inspect the equipment for hazards and discuss them with the owner.

4. Do not take unnecessary risks by walking on water features or rocks where you could fall off.

5. Show your customers how to operate their equipment—especially how to shut the pool off in an emergency.

6. Have the equipment and containers in your truck located where they cannot intermix, and spills cannot happen. Secure your chemical containers to avoid movement and shifting. Keep lids on the chemical containers tight and secure. Mark your containers to prevent using the wrong chemical. Never mix chemicals.

SAFETY EQUIPMENT

Because many deaths have resulted in lawsuits, residential pool safety has become more important for the homeowner. So many children drown every year that there should be a law requiring more safety equipment for the pool owner. Most planning departments require separate fencing and safety equipment for a pool. Most fences have to be over 48″ and the latch should be 54″ in height. Different areas have different codes for safety concerning a pool.

One of the best preventive pieces of equipment for pools is a "baby barrier." It is a custom fence that is built for each pool and has removable sections that can be entered in different places. Most have a very simple latch that a child cannot open since it takes some strength and coordination to unlock and open the gate. Most safety equipped locked gates open from the inside out, which also makes it difficult for a child to unlatch and open a gate with this system installed.

There are several different manufacturers and many types of safety barriers. The products that are sold in my location are installed only by trained installers from the factory to ensure that you get quality installations and to limit the liability to the company that manufactures them. They are a consideration when planning a pool, and if used properly they perform an excellent preventive measure. They have been designed to be very easy to use for the pool owner.

Another simple but effective device is an alarm for the door, gate, or pool. There are many manufacturers of these products and some work better than others. Door alarms are simple magnetic actuated devices that when the magnetic field is breached it activates an alarm notifying you that the door has been opened. They also make an alarm that mounts on a pool fence gate if it is opened. Some of these devices come with an option of a remote speaker or siren that you can install in your home. They are also a very wise investment.

Alarms are available that react to splashing and wave action in water. They were first introduced for on-the-ground pools. If someone enters the pool or there is water movement, it makes a certain noise, and it can also use a remote alarm.

There are safety nets that go over the surface of a pool like a leaf net. They are designed so that an infants' heads cannot be put through the netting, but the openings are large enough so that movement is difficult, limiting the child from crawling on the net.

A pool safety ring is a U.S. Coast Guard approved ring like a fat hula hoop that is designed to be a flotation device for rescuing people in water. Many companies make these rings but I recommend that you use only the ones that are Coast Guard approved. We found that they cost about $25 more than the unapproved versions.

No matter how you look at pool safety, the equipment is cheaper than a casket.

A safety hook attaches to a pool pole and is designed so you can hook an individual and pull him or her to safety. Special poles are available for this hook so that they do not pull apart when towing an object to the pool's edge.

Because of the recent drowning of children who were caught in suction drains, a new safety drain cover has been marketed that not only eliminates the chance for a child to be pulled by the vacuum of the drain, but also keeps long hair from being entangled in the drain.

The most common name is the "anti-hair and anti entrapment safety "cover", another piece of equipment that is well worth its investment.

A system that will soon be required to be safety device on all new pools is called a SVRS system or Safety Vacuum Release System. This system senses a restriction or interruption in the flow of water and shuts the pump off in milliseconds. I do have to admit that my personal experience is very limited in this area. I have only seen one pool that had this system installed, and the owners had no complaints. This technology, as well as others will be watched over time. Unfortunately, in this area it usually takes a drowning to get attention to safety measures.

There are many types of safety covers for pools. Some are put on manually, and some have automatic hydraulic systems that cover the pool and uncover it at the touch of a switch or key switch. These covers work very well and are safe. The problem with the covers is that you have to remove the water and debris from the top of the cover before you can open it up. A special cover pump should be used at all times that senses water on the surface of the cover and automatically turns on to remove the water. A heavy rainfall or loss of water can damage a cover. It partially relies on being able to sit on the surface of the water. Added weight such as rain can damage the cover or its track.

CHEMICAL TREATMENT CHARTS

There is a difference between liquid and dry measurements. Basic math skills are needed for calculations of pool water volume and chemical measurements. The only way to know the exact volume of water in a pool is to use a meter that tells you how much water has been added to a pool. Calculating volume by measurement is only an estimation. It is advised that you add fewer chemicals than you have estimated to ensure that you do not overdose the pool water. Upon retesting you can see how the pool reacts, and if your volume works with the amount of chemicals added. As previously stated it is always easier to add more than to take away. Before retesting, wait at least a full cycle of filtration or a day for the chemicals to be in solution. If you have added stabilizer or calcium, give it two or three days before retest to allow the chemicals to be absorbed adequately by the water. Stabilizer is especially slow to dissolve.

LIQUID (FLUID or VOLUME) MEASURMENTS (approximate)			
1 teaspoon		⅓ tablespoon	5 ml
1 tablespoon	½ ounce	3 teaspoons	15 ml
2 tablespoons	1 fluid ounce	⅛ cup, 6 teaspoons	30 ml
½ cup	4 fluid ounces	8 tablespoons	118 ml
1 cup	8 fluid ounces	16 tablespoons	237 ml
2 cups	16 fluid ounces	1 pint	473 ml
4 cups	32 fluid ounces	1 quart	946 ml, 0.946 liters
1 pint	16 fluid ounces	½ quart	473 ml
2 pints	32 fluid ounces	1 quart	946 ml, 0.946 liters
8 pints	1 gallon/ 128 fluid ounces		3785 ml, 3.78 liters
4 quarts	1 gallon/ 128 fluid ounces		3785 ml, 3.78 liters
1 liter	1.057 quarts		1000 ml
128 fluid ounces	1 gallon		3785 ml, 3.78 liters

DRY (WEIGHT) MEASUREMENTS (approximate)			
1 ounce		30 grams	
4 ounces	¼ pound	125 grams	
8 ounces	½ pound	240 grams	
12 ounces	¾ pound	375 grams	
16 ounces	1 pound	454 grams	
32 ounces	2 pounds	907 grams	
1 kilogram	2.2 pounds/ 35.2 ounces	1000 grams	

Chemicals vary in strength depending on the manufacturer and you should always read the label on the packaging. Let us say that the dosage for calcium hypochloride is 2 pounds at 63 percent available chlorine. The product that you have is 73 percent available chlorine. Here is how to figure the proper amount needed.

Sixty three (percentage called for) divided by 73 (actual percent of chlorine) times 2.0 (pounds needed) equals 1.726 or 1.73 pounds of Calcium Hypochlorite at a 73 percent strength. This mathematical solution can be used on the following chart.

AMOUNT OF CHLORINE TO INTRODUCE A 1 PPM CHLORINE LEVEL					
% Available Chlorine	400 gallons 1512 liters	1,000 gallons 3780 liters	5,000 gallons 18,900 liters	10,000 gal 37,800 liters	25,000 gal 94,500 liters
12.5 %	.41 fl oz	1.02 fl oz	5.1 fl oz	10.2 fl oz	27.2 fl oz
65%	0.08 oz	0.22 oz	1.03 oz	2.05 oz	5.0 oz
75%	0.07 oz	0.20 oz	0.95 oz	1.77 oz	4.33 oz
90%	0.06 oz	0.15 oz	0.74 oz	1.48 oz	3.60 oz

Bromine is different and since the bromine tablets usually weigh out at 18 grams, it is hard to calculate additional treatments for adjustments. This chart will show you the amount of sodium bromide (Yellow Treat) that it would take to raise the level of 1 ppm. This has to have an equal amount of chlorine or potassium monopersulfate to activate it. A spa with ozone will activate the bromine by itself.

AMOUNT OF BROMINE TO RAISE LEVEL 1	
300-400 GAL (1134-1512 LITERS)	2 GRAMS
450-500 GAL (1701-1870) LITERS)	3 GRAMS
1000 GAL (3780 LITERS)	6 GRAMS

Algae removal requires a 30 to 50 ppm chlorine level to kill algae depending on the type of algae you have. Super chlorination (break-point chlorination) usually is 10 times the normal amount to break up chloramines and bromamines. That is simple to calculate. Just multiply the amount of chlorine needed to provide a 2.5 chlorine level by 10, and that is the amount of chlorine you need. This chart shows the algae kill dosage for a 50 PPM level of chlorine.

50 PPM ALGAE KILL DOSAGE					
% Available Chlorine	400 gallons 1512 liters	1,000 gallons 3780 liters	5,000 gallons 18,900 liters	10,000 gal 37,800 liters	25,000 gal 94,500 liters
12.5%	20.5 oz	51 oz	2 gal	4 gal	10.6 gal
65%	4 oz	11 oz	3.2 lbs	6.4 lbs	15.6 lbs
75%	3.5 oz	10 oz	3 lbs	5.53 lbs	13.53 lbs
90%	3 oz	7.5 oz	2.3 lbs	4.6 lbs	11.25 lbs

Raising pH levels can be more accurately determined by using a Base Demand Test. This chart is a generic one that allows you to add the amount and then retest the next day. From this, you can adjust for the individual pool you are dealing with. A professional should use the Base Demand Test to add the correct amount so that they do not have to come back the next day.

TO RAISE PH USING SODA ASH (Sodium Carbonate, 100%)					
PH	400 gallons 1512 liters	1,000 gal 3,780 liters	5,000 gal 18,900 liters	10,000 gal 37,800 liters	25,000 gal 94,500 liters
7.2 – 7.4	10 grams	⅔ ounce	3 ounce	6 oz	1 lbs
7.0 –7.2	15 grams	¾ ounce	4 ounce	8 ounce	1 ¼ lbs
6.6 – 7.0	¾ ounce	1 ¼ ounce	6 ounce	12 ounce	2 lbs
Below 6.7	1 oz	1 ½ ounce	8 ounce	12 ounce	2 ½ lbs

Lowering pH is done with acid. Muriatic Acid (20 degree Baume'/31.45 percent HCI) is the main liquid used and sodium bisulfate 93.2 percent is a dry acid used. The professional test kit has an Acid Demand Test, which accurately tells you the proper dosage. The following charts are generic using both types of acid. Using the correct amount of acid is critical. Lowering the pH level too much can cause damage to the surface of the pool and dissolves metals. Bromine spas and pools are move critical since bromine is far more aggressive than chlorine.

TO DECREASE PH USING MURIATIC ACID					
PH	400 gallons 1512 liters	1,000 gal 3,780 liters	5,000 gal 18,900 liters	10,000 gal 37,800 liters	25,000 gal 94,500 liters
7.6 – 7.8	.5 oz	1 ¼ oz	6 oz	12 oz	1 quart
7.8 – 8.0	.6 oz	1 ½ oz	8 oz	2 cups	1 ¼ quart
8.0 –8.4	1 oz	2 ½ oz	12 oz	24 oz	2 quarts
Over 8.4	1 ¼ oz	3 oz	2 cups	1 quart	2 ½ quarts

TO DECREASE PH USING DRY ACID (Sodium Bisulfate)					
These dosages are estimated based on a certain chemical manufacturer and can differ from one manufacturer to another. Care must be used to establish the correct dosage.					
PH	400 gallons 1512 liters	1,000 gal 3,780 liters	5,000 gal 18,900 liters	10,000 gal 37,800 liters	25,000 gal 94,500 liters
7.6 –7.8	.5 oz	1.5 oz	7.5 oz	14 oz	2.3 lbs
7.8 – 8.0	.7 oz	1.75 oz	8.75 oz	17.5 oz	2.75 lbs
8.0 – 8.4	1.2 oz	3.5 oz	1 lbs	2 lbs	5 lbs
Over 8.4	1.5 oz	5 oz	1.5 lbs	3.0 lbs	7.5 lbs

TO LOWER TOTAL ALKALINITY USING MURIATIC ACID					
Reduce By	POOL	VOLUME			
PPM	400 Gallons 1,512 liters	1,000 Gal 3,780 liters	5,000 gal 18,900 liters	10,000 gal 37,800 liters	25,000 gal 94,500 liters
10	1 oz liquid	0.26 cup	1.3 cup	1.3 pints	3.25 pints
20	2 oz liquid	0.52 cup	1.3 pints	1.3 quarts	3.25 quarts
30	3 oz liquid	0.78 cup	1.5 pints	1.95 quarts	1.22 gallon
40	4 oz liquid	1.04 cup	1.3 quarts	2.6 quarts	1.63 gallon
50	5 oz liquid	1.3 cup	1.63 quarts	3.25 quarts	2.03 gallon
60	6 liquid oz	1.5 cup	2.0 quarts	1 gallon	2.5 gallon
70	7 liquid oz	1.9 cup	2.3 quarts	1.2 gallon	3 gallon
80	8 liquid oz	1 pint	2.5 quarts	1.25 gallon	3.25 gallon

TO LOWER TOTAL ALKALINITY USING MURIATIC ACID					
Reduce By	POOL	VOLUME			
90	9 liquid oz	1.2 pints	3 quarts	1.5 gallon	3.75 gallon

Using sodium bisulfate to lower alkalinity is not really cost effective. If the dry acid is used for safety measures, then a product called Pool Acid that consists of sulfuric acid can be substituted using the above chart. It will lower total alkalinity but has no cleaning properties. It does not have the strong odor of Muriatic Acid and is safer to use.

TO RAISE TOTAL ALKALINITY USING SODIUM BICARBONATE (Baking Soda)					
Increase by	POOL	VOLUME			
PPM	400 Gallons 1,512 liters	1,000 Gal 3,780 liters	5,000 gal 18,900 liters	10,000 gal 37,800 liters	25,000 gal 94,500 liters
10	1 ounce	2.5 ounces	.75 lbs	1.5 lbs	3.75 lbs
20	1.5 ounce	5 ounces	1.5 lbs	3.0 lbs	7.5 lbs
30	2 ounce	.5 lbs	2.25 lbs	4.5 lbs	11.25
40	2.5 ounce	10 ounces	3.00 lbs	6.0 lbs	15 lbs
60	5 ounce	.9 lbs	4.5 lbs	9.0 lbs	22.54 lbs
70	6 ounce	1 lbs	5.25 lbs	10.5 lbs	26.65 lbs
80	8 ounce	1.2 lbs	6.0 lbs	12.0 lbs	30.00 lbs
90	9 ounce	1.35 lbs	6.75 lbs	13.5 lbs	33.75
100	10 ounce	1.5 lbs	7.5 lbs	15.0 lbs	37.5 lbs

Raising calcium hardness has a different procedure from adding other chemicals. When water is introduced to calcium chloride dihydrate, it reacts very strong and creates heat. If you were to put two pounds of calcium chloride in a plastic bucket and add water, you would feel a lot of heat on the bottom of the bucket from the chemical reaction that is taking place.

The proper way to add calcium chloride is to dissolve two pounds of chemical in a bucket of water. When it is dissolved, pour it into pool around the sides. Continue this procedure after waiting 10 minutes until you have added 10 pounds of calcium chloride. Wait one hour before adding any more. Never pour calcium chloride on the bottom of the pool and especially on a vinyl liner. The time between additions of calcium chloride gives water a chance to absorb the product and put it in solution. Too much at one time could plug your filter media and may scale.

Figuring the amount of calcium chloride really does not require a chart. It is very simple.

For every 10 ppm of increase needed, you add two ounces of calcium chloride for 1,000 gallons of water volume.

Example:
We have a 20,000 gallon pool and we want to raise the level of hardness 80 ppm. Since the volume is 20 times the amount of the formula, you multiply 20 times 8 (the ppm you wish to raise divided by 10 ppm). That is 160. You then multiply 160 by 2 (ounces of product) and get 320. Since there are 16 ounces in a pound, you divide 320 by 16 and it comes out to 20 pounds of calcium chloride.

Calcium Chloride is one of the products that is better if you add a little less at first and then retest to make sure you did not add too much. This is in case your estimation of the volume of water in the pool is not accurate. The way to remove excess hardness from pool water is to drain some of the water and replace with new water. As previously stated, it is always easier to add more than to take away.

For safety, I have included this chart for calcium hardness

Increase PPM	1,000 Gallons	5,000 Gallons	10,000 Gallons	25,000 Gallons
10	2 oz	10 oz	1 lbs 4 oz	3 lbs 2 oz
20	4 oz	1 lbs 4 oz	2 lbs 8 oz	6 lbs 4 oz
30	6 oz	1 lbs 14 oz	3 lbs 12 oz	9 lbs 6 oz
40	8 oz	2 lbs 8 oz	5 lbs	12 lbs 8 oz
50	10 oz	3 lbs 2 oz	6 lbs 4 oz	15 lbs 10 oz
60	12 oz	3 lbs 12 oz	7 lbs 8 oz	18 lbs 12 oz
70	14 oz	4 lbs 6 oz	8 lbs 12 oz	21 lbs 14 oz
80	16 oz	5 lbs	10 lbs	25 lbs
90	1 lbs 2 oz	5 lbs 10 oz	11 lbs 4 oz	27 lbs 8 oz
100	1 lbs 4 oz	6 lbs 4 oz	12 lbs 8 oz	31 lbs 4 oz

Cyanuric acid is another product that if the level is too high you have to drain the pool. The formula for cyanuric acid is the same as calcium except the required dose to raise 10 ppm for 1,000 gallons of volume is 1.3 ounce. Due to the problems of adding too much cyanuric acid this chart will guide for proper dosages.

PPM Increase	1,000 gallons 1,512 liters	5,000 gallons 18,900 liters	10,000 gallons 37,800 liters	25,000 gallons 94,500 liters
10	1.3 oz	6.5 oz	13 oz	32.5 oz
20	2.6 oz	13 oz	26 oz	65 oz
30	3.9 oz	19.5 oz	39 oz	97.5 oz
40	5.2 oz	26 oz	52 oz	130 oz
50	6.5 oz	32.5 oz	65 oz	162.5 oz

Author Biography

Dan J. Hardy was born August 16, 1953, in Hereford, TX. His background in pool maintenance began on his dad's country club in Clovis, NM, in 1976. Ten years later, he opened his own business delivering and setting up spas and doing pool work at pre-manufactured homes in Albuquerque, NM.

He moved to Ocala, FL, in 1998 and opened Dan's Perfect Pool Service, Pool Palace, Mount View Enterprises, LLC, and then D & C Enterprises.

In 2006 he Joined Rick Lorick Construction to train pool and service technicians to maintain high end pools, performing mechanical service and repair.

He has worked on many fabulous pools for celebrities in Ocala including John Travolta and Kelly Preston; Terri Jones-Thayer, former Miss World and Revlon's perfect Charlie girl; and Brock Marion, a former Dallas Cowboy. "I also get to rub shoulders with

Ricky 'The Rocket' Nattiel, former Denver Bronco, on occasion at the office," Dan said.

Dan graduated from Boys Ranch High School in 1971, Boys Ranch Texas near Amarillo, TX, and from General Motors Technical School in Oklahoma City, OK, in 1972. He attended Amarillo Vocational College for Auto Mechanics and studied mechanical engineering at Tacoma Community College, Tacoma, WA.

Besides a career as a pool professional, Dan is a licensed Realtor® in Florida and a partner with his wife, Carol, in Real Estate for Keller Williams Cornerstone Realty.

He has two daughters, Randi and Marci, and two sons, Matthew and Michael. His pride is his grandson, Austin Shane.

Glossary of Terms

ACID: An acid whether liquid or dry that has the ability to lower pH and alkalinity in water. Also muriatic acid can be used to acid wash a pool and remove unwanted stains and scale from pool surfaces.

ACID DEMAND: A test that determines the amount of acid that is required to lower the pH in water.

ACID RAIN: Rain having an unusual low pH usually 4.5 or lower, which is caused by pollutants in the atmosphere.

ACID WASH: Describes using a mixture of Muriatic Acid and water at different ratios to achieve the cleaning of plaster on your pool surface.

ACRYLIC: A material that is usually formed by heat and a mold using vacuum to form an object. Portable spas are made of acrylic.

AERATOR: A vented pipe installed in the plumbing mainly in spas that can have an adjustment of air that is introduced into a water line before returning to the body of water.

AIR RELIEF VALVE: A valve that is located on a spa or pool filter that allows you to remove the air that is trapped so that it does not cloud the water.

AIR BLOWER: A fan type motor that forces air into a spa for agitation of the water.

AIR SWITCH: Mostly on spas and in-home whirlpool baths that allow you to turn it on by pushing an air button that activates a switch in another location to turn on equipment such as pumps and blowers. They come in single or multiple functions.

ALGAE: Microscopic living planta or plant like organisma of over 21,000 different varieties. Normal pool algae are either green, yellow, or black, with an additional form of alga that is called pink and is not a real alga at all but a bacterium. These organisms usually grow in water or on surfaces and can become airborne to contaminate other water sources. Some are chlorine resistant and are hard to kill.

ALGAECIDE: CIDE means to kill. Algaecides are designed to kill algae and aid in the prevention of reoccurrences of them.

ALGAESTAT: An algaestat retards and prevents growth of algae. Some algaecides are only algaestats and should be looked at very carefully.

ALGAE SPORES: Dormant algae residing in atmospheric conditions, which are introduced into the pool or spa by rain, winds, and dust storms.

ALKALINE: When water has a pH of 7.0 or higher.

ALKALINITY: Alkalinity refers to the water in an above acidic state. Above a pH of 7.0. Acts as a buffer for pH and aids in controlling the correct pH in normal recommended parameters. Aids in the prevention spiking of pH levels.

ALUMINUM SULFATE: Sometimes called a clarifier, the main ingredient ALUM gathers smaller particles together and makes larger particles. These particles are dropped to the bottom of the pool and are usually vacuumed to waste so that they don't re-enter the pool. Also known as flocculants, they are mainly used as a last resort to clear cloudy water and to remove unwanted particles in water.

AMBIENT TEMPERATURE: The temperature of the surrounding atmosphere.

ANSI: American National Standards Institute. Sets construction standards.

APHA: American Public Standards Association. National public health and safety organization.

AMMONIA: Very soluble combination of nitrogen and hydrogen NH3 that when introduced in pool water at certain levels can tie up free chlorine levels to make chloramines and in bromine pools and spas make bromamines that makes the sanitizers very weak and ineffective.

AMPERAGE (AMPS): The measurement of electricity that equals watts divided by voltage.

ANTI SIPHON VALVE: A valve designed to stop the flow of water going back to a certain source.

ANTISURGE VALVE: A check valve that is used in pool and spa plumbing to prevent water from entering the blower assembly.

ANTIVORTEX: Commonly used in the description of a main drain cover in a pool or spa to limit the whirlpool effect when water is pulled through it.

ASCORBIC ACID: A compound that removes iron stains from vinyl liners and fiberglass pools and spas.

AVAILABLE CHLORINE: Free chlorine that is readily available to sanitize water and that is not locked up with ammonia.

BACKWASH: The reversal of water in filters to remove unwanted particles and clean the filter so that flow is established to a proper level for the removal of contaminants.

BACTERIA: Dangerous micro-organisms that may be introduced in pool water and can be very dangerous to the health of humans.

BALANCED WATER: Balanced water is having all your chemical parameters where they should be, and in balance of each other. Total alkalinity, calcium hardness, temperature, and pH, as measured using the Langelier Index of water balance equals zero.

BALL VALVE: A valve that has a ball in the center with a sized hole through it so that flow can be controlled.

BASE: Chemicals of an alkaline nature, which will counteract the pH of an acid.

BASE DEMAND: A test used to determine proper amounts of base to raise the pH of pool water, which could be soda ash (sodium carbonate) or sodium bicarbonate if alkalinity needs to be raised.

BIGUANIDES: Sanitizers using the polymer PHMB, a non-halogen sanitizer for pool and spa use. Common names of products are Soft Swim and Baquacil. However, this peroxide base chemical cannot kill algae alone.

BLOWER: A device that blows air through piping to give spa jets a bubbling effect.

BONDING: The connecting of the pool shell reinforcement rod, the light, and all metal construction materials to prevent electrolysis. All tie together and are grounded by a rod inserted in the ground.

BREAKPOINT CHLORINATION: Also called shocking. It is adding an amount of chlorine to a chlorinated pool to destroy chloramines, which is a combination of chlorine and ammonia that comes from sweat and urine of large bather loads in the pool. Chloramines tie up free available chlorine that is ineffective as a sanitizer. A recommended dose of 30 to 50 ppm will not only destroy chloramines but will also kill most algae.

BROADCASTING: Dispensing of chemicals by throwing them over the vast portion of the surface of the water.

BROMAMINES: Combined bromine and ammonia with the ability to sanitize unlike chlorine.

BROMINE: A member of the halogen family, commonly used as a sanitizer in spas, due to its resistance to hot water. Not commonly used in pools due to its cost and is unstable and highly aggressive if water balance is not kept with in parameters.

BTU: British Thermal Unit. It is the amount of heat required to raise one pound of water one degree Fahrenheit.

BUFFER: A base such as sodium bicarbonate, which resists sudden changes in pH called spiking.

BY PASS: An arrangement of valves designed to redirect the flow of water to a piece of equipment. They are also used to control flow to a certain equipment part or device.

CALCIUM: Mineral that is typically found in water as well as in other things. A metal ion in water which can form salts such as calcium carbonate causing cloudiness and/or scaling. Can be caused by an imbalance of pH.

CALCIUM BLEED: For pools, it is when the calcium leaches from the plaster. Normal on new surfaces but can be extreme if balance is not correct.

CALCIUM CARBONATE: Scale. A major component that is precipitated from the water and becomes attached to pool surfaces and to equipment and piping. Levels can rise due to the addition of calcium in many forms. Salt pools have a higher TDS of calcium as well as hard water sources. The use of calcium hypochlorite also adds to this level of hardness.

CALCIUM CHLORIDE: A salt used to raise levels of calcium hardness in your pool and spa water.

CALCIUM HARDNESS: The level of the mineral calcium dissolved in the pool water.

CALCIUM HYPOCHLORITE: Commonly called cal hypo or HTH. A granular form of chlorine that comes in different strengths of total chlorine. Adds to TDS but is fairly safe to use. Is an unstable form of chlorine. Cannot be mixed with any other chemical because of danger of chemical explosion. Addition of acid to cal hypo will result in chlorine gas, which can be lethal.

CARBON DIOXIDE: A gas, which when present in the water usually feeds algae growth and is introduced in several forms. Algae thrive on carbon dioxide.

CAUSTIC: Capable of eating or destroying by chemical action.

CAVITATION: When the discharge of the pump either exceeds the suction of the pump or a restriction causes the vacuum to collapse from the impeller of the pump. Can be caused by a clogged impeller.

CHITIN: A naturally occurring polymer found in the shells of crabs and lobsters. Contained in the product made by Vanson called Sea-Klear, chitin is a coagulant for oils, metals, and organic materials. Makes the small particles combine together to make larger particles that can be taken out by the filter.

CHELATOR: A chelating agent is a water soluble molecule that can bond tightly with metal ions, keeping them from coming out of suspension and depositing their stains and scale onto pool surfaces and equipment. Keeps metals in solution so that the filter can remove them.

CHECK VALVE: A device that lets water flow in one direction but not in the other direction.

CHLORAMINES: The combination of chlorine and ammonia or nitrogen that when combined creates a very unwanted odor and limits the sanitizing ability of chlorine.

CHLORINE: A member of the halogen family of sanitizers. It is available in liquid, gas, or granular forms of different strengths. Some are stabilized and some are unstable.

CHLORINE, AVAILABLE: Residual chlorine or chlorine that is available to destroy bacteria on contact.

CHLORINE DEMAND: Amount of free available chlorine that is demanded or needed by the water to raise the residue of chlorine to a certain level.

CHLORINE LOCK: It applies to chloramines that have no ability to sanitize properly and need to be shocked to release the chlorine in a free state. Also called breakpoint chlorination.

CHLORINE NEUTRALIZER: A chemical that makes chlorine useless or neutral.

CIRCULATION PUMP: In relationship to pools, the pump that circulates water for a particular purpose in the system.

CLARIFIER: A product that attracts small particles in the water so they become larger particles so the filter can properly remove them.

CONTAMINANTS: Described as making water unfit for use by the introduction of unwholesome or undesirable elements that can cause cloudiness of the water.

COPING: The top part of the pool that ties the pool and the deck together. Usually has an overhang and can be made of brick, concrete, pavers, wood, or plastic.

COPPER: A good algaecide. Copper as elemental is used in many pool products as an algaecide that when used properly kills all forms of algae. Can stain surfaces if not properly used.

COPPER SULFATE: Nicknamed Bluestone. A granular substance that is used to kill algae and also has a flocking ability.

CONDITIONER: Commonly called stabilizer. Usually cyanuric acid that slows the decomposition of chlorine products.

CORROSION: Wearing away of metal objects gradually in degrees usually as the result in a chemical action. A chemical reaction caused by unbalanced water, which causes metals or minerals to dissolve.

CORROSION RESISTANT: The ability of maintaining original surface characteristics under prolonged use.

CYANURIC ACID: Stabilizes pool water so that the residue of chlorine is not affected as much by the sun. Not needed in indoor pools. Not used with bromine products.

CYCLE: The completion of running the pool pump by turning over all the water in the pool in eight to ten hours. From start to stop is one cycle.

DEAD ZONE: An area in the pool that has poor or no circulation that allows particles to cling to the wall and floor. These areas will usually be the first to get a bloom of algae.

DECK: The area that surrounds the pool. Can be made of many materials.

DEFOAMER: A product that is designed to remove the foam on the surface of the water in a spa.

DIATOMACEOUS EARTH (DE): A light friable siliceous material derived mainly from diatoms (colonial algae) of skeletal remains. The white powder used in DE filters as a filter media to filter out very small particles.

DICHLOR: Sodium Dichloro-s-triazinetrione. A very soluble form of chlorine that easily dissolves and is stabilized. Excellent sanitizer but the cost makes the use of it unpopular. It is fast dissolving, will not cloud the water, and has a long shelf life. The second most expensive chlorine on the market. Care should be taken when shocking a pool with dichlor due to the addition of stabilizer that is mixed in with the chlorine. It has a pH very close to seven (neutral).

DIFFUSER: A component inside a pool circulation pump that actually slows down the flow of water to make it more stable and increase pressure. Covers the impeller and has slots, holes, or veins that precisely control the flow of water.

DPD: Diethy-phenylene diamene. A method of testing chlorine levels in the pool water. DPD test allows for the determination of total and free available chlorine levels.

DRY ACID: Sodium bisulfate, a granular form of acid. Mostly used in spas or by elderly pool and spa owners. Safer to use and distribute. Adjustment for pH and alkalinity.

EFFECTIVE FILTRATION AREA: The total surface of a medium where the designed flow rate will be maintained during filtration.

ELECTROLYSIS: Two or more dissimilar metals passing

through water with an electrical current. Causes light rings to turn black and can stain surfaces.

ELEMENT: The actual filter inside the filter body that traps the small particles of unwanted debris in water.

ENZYMES: Enzymes are complex proteins that cause a specific chemical change in other substances without being changed themselves. A product used in pools to remove scum, odors, the ring around the water line that consists of oils, make-up, and by-products that contaminate pool water and make it cloudy. Also good for cleaning filter elements. Most dishwashing liquids have enzymes in them to dissolve these by-products.

EPA: The Environmental Protection Agency.

FIBER OPTICS: A light used in pools and spas that have a source that is not near the water and lends the light down the fiber optic cable which illuminates wherever it is exposed.

FILTER: Probably the most important part of a pool and spa system that is designed to remove unwanted particles in the water. Filters vary in the size of particles that they can remove.

FIRE UP: A term used by the pool industry that starts the treatment of water on a new pool or one that has been drained. Usually consists of basic water chemistry and shocking the new water to kill bacteria and regulate the levels of chemistry to protect a new surface during curing.

FOAMING: Bubbles. The reaction to soaps, oils, and other by products that makes thick bubbles over the surface of the pool or spa water. Mostly in spas with the small volume of water. Some algaecides and algaestats create foaming.

FLOCCULANT: A product that acts as a clarifier by attracting the smaller particles and combining them in larger particles that drop to the bottom of the pool to allow you to vacuum them to waste.

FLOW RATE: The volume of water measured in gallons in the United States that describes the amount of water passing through an object.

FREE CHLORINE: The available chlorine residue that is not tied up with any other element that is available for sanitizing water. The level after the demand is satisfied.

GPM: Gallons per minute

GROUND FAULT INTERRUPTER: Commonly called a GFI. A device that is designed to interrupt the electrical flow to aid in the prevention of electrocution.

HALOGEN: The family of elements such as bromine, chlorine, fluorine, and iodine that are considered oxidizing (sanitizers) agents.

HAMMERHEAD: A piece of equipment for vacuuming a pool that has an electric motor in it to pull debris from the bottom of the pool and up into a containment bag.

HARD WATER: The term of a high calcium level in pool and spa water caused by calcium and magnesium.

HEATER: A piece of equipment used on spas and pools that raises the temperature of water to a desired limit. Pool heaters can be wood fired, electric, oil, and gas powered units.

HEAT EXCHANGER: The part of the heater that absorbs the heat and distributes it to the water for raising the temperature of the water in a pool or spa.

HEAT PUMP: A piece of equipment that removes the heat from the air and transfers it to pool water.

HORSEPOWER: Ratings of pool motors and equipment. It takes 746 watts of electricity to make one horsepower. One horsepower is the power it would take to raise 550 pounds to one foot in one second.

HYDRATION: A product of adding some type of moisture to a dry substance that combines to become one.

IMPELLER: A part of a centrifugal pump that is connected to the shaft of the armature in an electric motor that rotates at a set speed (usually 3600 RPMs). It flows water and creates a suction in the intake line drawing water to the pump.

IMPURITIES: Any substance dissolved or suspended in water which alters the chemical and /or physical properties of the pure substance.

IODINE: A sanitizer for water that is not commonly used in pools. Member of the halogen family is commonly used in the purification of drinking water. Kills bacteria and prevents algae growth. Can stain surfaces.

IONIZER: An ionizer is a device that is in either a light form or injection. The injection is usually by dissolving metal such as copper by an electrical charge and dissolving it in pool water. An ionizer works as an electric algaecide.

IRON: Iron is usually introduced into a pool or spa either by the source water or by something that is metal that has been in contact with the water. Chemicals can be used to keep the iron in solution and remove it from surfaces and let the filter take them out. Iron can be seen on the returns and main drain covers first and should be treated. Letting metals go without treatment can stain the surface of the pool so that even with acid washing will not remove them.

LANGELIER INDEX: The Langelier Saturation Index is a means of evaluating water quality information to determine if the water is corrosive or scale forming. Even with water being close to the zero rating (neutral) which is balanced water, corrosion can still be occurring.

LATERALS: The tubes in the bottom of a sand filter, which takes in the filtered water for the return to the pool. During a backwash, the water is reversed and comes through the laterals and forces water up through the sand to wash the particles from the sand to the waste port to be removed from the filter.

LEAF EATER: A cleaning tool that hooks up to a water hose and has a small micron bag to collect debris in a pool. The water is shot through small holes in the opening of the cleaner shooting water upwards at an angle causing suction. This sucks debris into the bag to be removed from the pool. Works great on leaves. There are two models. One has wheels for concrete pools and the other has a brush that goes around the bottom of the cleaner for vinyl pools.

LEAF RAKE: A large net that hooks to a pool pole that is deep in design and is used to skim the surface of a pool or remove debris from the bottom of the pool. Different sizes are available to remove either standard debris or fine micron nets to remove small debris.

LITHIUM HYPOCHLORITE: Chemical formula LIOCI is produced by bubbling chlorine gas through a solution of lithium, sodium, and potassium sulphates. Can be used directly on vinyl pools. It dissolves very rapidly. It is an unstable form of chlorine that requires stabilizer. It is the most expensive of the halogen family.

MAGNESIUM: A dissolved mineral in water. Contributes to water hardness and turbidity.

MAIN DRAIN: The drain or multiple drains in the bottom of a pool or the side of a fiberglass pool or spa that is an intake for the water in the lower section of the water to circulate water. Without a main drain, the lower section of a deep pool can become a dead zone, which would be a perfect breeding ground for algae.

MARCITE: A product that is used as a plaster for the surface of a pool. Most marcite products contain no marble aggregates.

MEDIA: A substance that is used primarily in a DE filter to act as the filtering component that gathers small debris and when is saturated can be back-washed out of the filter for the addition of new media.

MISSION CLAMP: A device with a rubber inner section and a stainless steel outer section. Clamps surround the stainless steel portion to be tightened up to secure a watertight connection in a repair. Can be the same size pipe or they make them for different sizes of pipes to be connected. Can be used on different kinds of pipes.

MICRON: A measurement that equals one millionth of a meter. .000394 of an inch.

MICROORGANISM: A living, breathing creature in your pool. The reason a sanitizer has to be used in pool water.

MURIATIC ACID: The liquid dilution of Hydrochloric Acid used to lower pH and alkalinity. Can be used as a cleaning agent for concrete, bricks, scale, and irons. Can also be used to remove the calcium and metal buildup on cartridge and DE filters.

NEGATIVE EDGE: A feature that is built on one or more walls of the pool to let the water overflow to another container. It gives the appearance of water extending to the horizon and self cleans the surface of the pool of debris floating on the surface.

N.S.F.: National Sanitation Foundation

NITROGEN: When combined with chlorine, nitrogen creates chloramines. Nitrogen can be found in swimmer wastes, such as perspiration, suntan oil, hair tonics.

NONCHLORINE SHOCK: A granular form of potassium monopersulfate. An oxidizer that acts as a catalyst to activate sodium bromide. Breaks up chloramines and bromamines but cannot kill algae.

ORGANIC: A naturally occurring material such as perspiration, urine, oils, and plant material to include leaves and bark.

OTO: Another method of testing for free available chlorine levels in your pool. Not believed to be as accurate as DPD.

OXIDIZER: Chemicals that release chlorine are among the group of chemicals classified as "oxidizers." These chemicals are in the halogen family along with peroxides and persulfates.

OZONATOR: A device that uses oxygen to make ozone that is delivered in a pool or spa.

OZONE: The molecule containing three atoms of oxygen; known to be a very powerful sanitizer. Ozone equipment creates this molecule by UV radiation or by discharge generators.

PARTS PER MILLION (PPM): A measurement used to calculate the "parts per million" or "pounds per million pounds" of chemicals and compounds in your pool water.

PH: The scale of relative acidity or alkalinity to soil or water. From a scale of 0 to 14 (7.0 being neutral). Below 7.0 is acidic and above is alkaline.

POTASSIUM PERMONOSULFATE: See nonchlorine shock.

POLYMER: An algaecide/algaestat made up of repeating polymer molecules. Primarily used for green algae.

PPM: Parts per million. A measurement of chemical concentrations of chemicals in the water. For example, alkalinity should be kept at 80-120 parts per million, by weight and in relation to the water it's dissolved in.

PRECIPITATION: To precipitate is to come out of solution; become insoluble by result of chemical action. Material forced out of solution, purposefully or accidentally, will then settle, stain, scale, or remain suspended in the water.

PRESSURE SWITCH: A switch that can be activated by pressure. Can work in the reverse way that if no pressure is exerted, the device is not activated. Can be used as a safety switch also.

PRESSURE GAUGE: A device that shows the pressure of the water in a system. Usually mounted on the filter.

PRIMING: The starting of a flow of water to the suction side of a pump. As water flows to the pressure side of the pump, suction is increased until the limits of the pump have been met.

PSI: Pounds per square inch. The measurement of pressure on a unit.

PVC: Poly Vinyl Chloride. A plastic type product that is used for pipe, fittings, and pieces of equipment. Chemical and sun resistant and can handle a lot of pressure. Has good strength for its weight.

QUATERNARY AMMONIUM COMPOUND: A type of algaestat composed of ammonia compounds. Commonly called Quats.

RATE OF TURNOVER: The time that it takes to circulate the entire amount of water in a pool or spa.

REAGENT: Chemical indicators used in testing water balance. Can be liquid, powder, or tablets.

RESIDUAL: Refers to free available chlorine levels that remain in the pool.

SANITIZER: A chemical agent used to oxidize bacteria.

SCALE: Mineral salts that are forced out of solution. Scaling condition is deposits that attach themselves to surfaces and fixtures in the pool. Can plug or restrict the flow of water if severe.

SEDIMENT: A solid material that has come out of solution in water.

SEQUESTERING AGENT: A chemical that locks up minerals so that they stay in solution where the filter can take them out.

SERVICE FACTOR: A rating for the efficiency of an electric motor. One horsepower is equivalent to 746 watts of power.

SHOCK: See Breakpoint Chlorination

SODA ASH: Sodium carbonate. Has a pH of 11.3 and reduces the acidic conditions of water. Used to raise the pH in water.

SODIUM BICARBONATE (baking soda): Has a pH of 8.3. Used to raise the alkalinity in a pool.

SODIUM BISULFATE: See Dry Acid

SODIUM HYPOCHLORITE: Liquid chlorine used in pools. pH of 12.95 and comes in different strengths. Liquid chlorine for pools average 11.5 percent available chlorine. Very corrosive.

SODIUM TETRABORATE: Borax. Sodium Tetraborate Decahydrate. The product you buy in grocery stores. Sodium Tetraborate Pentahydrate. Used for pools. Dissolved in water the two substances are identical. Is an EPA approved Algaestat under the name of Proteam Supreme. Can also be used to raise pH without affecting Alkalinity.

SODIUM DICHLOR: A granular form of stabilized chlorine. Used super-chlorination.

SOFT WATER: Water that has a low calcium and/or magnesium content.

SOLAR HEAT: The heating system on a pool that absorbs the heat of the sun and ambient temperature to heat water by passing it through panels or chambers usually mounted on roofs.

SOLAR COVER: A cover that sits directly on top of the water of a spa or pool and resists the leakage of temperature and evaporation. Used with Solar Heat and with normal heating.

STABILIZER: See Cyanuric Acid.

STRAINER: The basket located inside the trap of a pump that removes larger debris before it enters the pump and the filter.

SUPERCHLORINATION: Applying seven to ten times the normal amounts of chlorine to the pool as an added "boost" for contaminant removal. Some refer to super-chlorinating as being less than shocking, in that breakpoint levels are not reached.

TEST STRIPS: Chemical reagent strips that accurately test water for various chemicals if an interference of a high chemical does not affect them.

TITRATION: A method of testing for total alkalinity, calcium hardness, and acid/base demand. By adding a certain titrate the liquid reacts and changes colors.

TOTAL ALKALINITY: The "buffering" capacity of the water. Resist sudden changes or spikes in pH levels. Total alkalinity is the amount of alkaline substances that measure above a pH 7.0.

TOTAL DISSOLVED SOLIDS (TDS): A measure of everything that has ever dissolved in the water; all the matter that is in solution. High TDS levels can over-saturate your water. TDS is removed by draining pool water.

TURBIDITY: Cloudy, dull, hazy water.

VANISHING EDGE: See negative edge.

VENTURI: A part that is restricted in the center and opening up on the ends that when water is forced through it, the force of the water creates a vacuum. Usually found with older chlorine systems and ozone generators.

WATER FEATURE: A design made out of rocks, a series of rocks, a waterfall, or any other design that is part of the pool and lets water flow over them to the pool for an unusual and enjoyable look.

WINTERIZING: The service of getting a pool ready for winter months to prevent damage and freezing of the pool and equipment.

WEIR: A part that fits into a skimmer that is hinged and regulates the amount of water that flows over the top of the weir and only lets the debris on the top of the water enter for proper skimming. Also can be a floating weir that is a cylinder shaped object in a skimmer basket that also performs the same function.

Index

A

B

C

D

E

F

G

H

T

U

V

W

Y